VIZ PRESENTS

SID the SEXIST

THE JOY OF SEXISM

THE JOY OF SEXISM

Editor Simon Donald

Written, Designed and Illustrated
by Simon Donald, Graham Dury and Simon Thorp

Additional illustration by
Steve Donald
and Simon Ecob

Photography by
Colin Davison

Production Editor and Sex Traitor
Sheila Thompson

Production Team Assistant
Susan Patterson

A Hoose of Viz Production
PO Box 1PT, Newcassel upon Tyne, NE99 1PT

ISBN 1 870870 93 X

Published in Great Britain by John Broon Publishing Ltd., The Burt Hoose,
Crabtree Lane, Fulham, London SW6 6LU.

SID the SEXIST
featuring BAZ, BOB *and* JOE
in a feature length farrago of filth
For Whom The Bells Toll

CONTINUED ON PAGE 12

Worst woman driver

THE SEXIST BOOK OF RECORDS

Softest porn

Largest toaster

Biggest fart

Most pencils

Car Parking
The smallest kerbside space successfully reversed into by a woman was one of 19.36m *63 ft 2 ins*, equivalent to three standard parking spaces by Mrs. Elizabeth Simpkins (GB) driving an unmodified Vauxhall Nova 'Swing' on the 12th October 1993. She started the manoeuvre at 11.15am in Ropergate, Pontefract and successfully parked within three feet of the pavement 8 hours 14 mins later. There was slight damage to the bumpers and wings of her own and the two adjoining cars, as well as a shop frontage and two lamp posts.

The World of Women

Driving

Car repairs
The largest bill for fictitious work carried out on a woman's car by garage mechanics was one of £6322.88 charged by Joskin Bros, Motors Ltd. of Stevenage. Calling in for a routine service on her one year old Peugeot 305, Mrs. June Spears agreed to pay for, amongst other things, new trumpets (£752), cracked Gangle pin (£1785), realignment of main glib shaft (£2268), new grommets (£112), set of hexagonal Tag nuts and dangleberry adapter (£35) and new piss-take valves (£120). No work was actually carried out on the car during the six weeks it spent at the garage but 4000 miles was put on the clock and she later received a speeding summons from Italian police.

Traffic light cosmetics
The longest spell spent oblivious to traffic lights whilst applying make up was one of 1 hr 51 mins 38 secs by Ms. Janet Dodson (GB) at a road junction in the centre of Preston on the 1st August 1975. Ms. Dodson, a piano teacher, beautified herself through 212 cycles of the lights, creating a tailback of irate motorists stretching 28 miles towards Leeds.

Incorrect Driving ● Dr. Julie Thorn and the Saab 900 in which she made her record breaking drive on 2nd April 1987.

Incorrect Driving
The longest journey completed with the handbrake on was one of 504 Km *313 miles* from Stranraer to Holyhead by Dr. Julie Thorn (GB) at the wheel of a Saab 900 on the 2nd April 1987. Dr. Thorn smelled burning two miles into her journey at Aird but pressed on to Holyhead with smoke billowing from the rear wheels. This journey also holds the records for the longest completed with the choke fully out and the right indicator flashing.

Traffic light cosmetics ● A section of the 28 mile grid lock caused by Janet Dodson in August 1975.

Shopping

Shop Dithering
The longest time spent dithering in a shop was 12 days between 21st August and 2nd September 1995 by Mrs. Sandra Wilks (GB) in the Birmingham branch of Dorothy Perkins. Entering the shop on a Saturday morning, Mrs.

Wilks could not choose between two near identical dresses which were both in the sale. After one hour, her husband, sitting on a chair by the changing room with his head in his hands, told her to buy both. Mrs. Wilks eventually bought the one for £12.99, only to return the next day and buy the other one. To date, she has yet to wear it.
Mrs. Wilks also holds the record for window shopping longevity, when, starting on September 12th 1995, she stood motionless gazing at a pair of shoes in Clinkard's window in Kiddeminster for 3 weeks 2 days before eventually going home.

Jumble Sale Massacre
The greatest number of old ladies to perish whilst fighting at a jumble sale is 98, at a Methodist Church Hall in Castleford, West Yorkshire on February 12th 1991. When the doors opened at 10.00am, the initial scramble to get in cost 16 lives, a further 25 being killed in a crush at the first table. A seven-way skirmish then broke out over a pinafore dress costing 10p which escalated into a full scale melee resulting in another 18 lives being lost. A pitched battle over a headscarf then ensued and quickly spread throughout the hall claiming 39 old women. The jumble sale raised £5.28 for local boy scouts.

Social

Talking about Nothing
Mrs. Mary Caterham (GB) and Mrs. Marjorie Steele (GB) sat in a kitchen in Blackburn, Lancs. and talked about nothing whatsoever for four and a half months from 1st May to the 17th August 1978, pausing only for coffee, cakes and toilet visits. Throughout the whole time, no information was exchanged and neither woman gained any new knowledge whatsoever.
The outdoor record for talking about nothing is held by Mrs. Vera Etherington (GB) and her neighbour Mrs. Dolly Booth (GB) of Ipswich, who between 11th November 1983 and 12th January 1984 chundered on over their fence in an unenlightening dialogue lasting 62 days until Mrs. Booth remembered she'd left the bath running.

Gossiping
On February 18th 1992, Joyce Blatherwick, a close friend of Mrs. Agnes Banbury (GB) popped round for a cup of tea and a chat, during the course of which she told Mrs.

Jumble sale massacre ● The Revd. Julian Spriggs helps one of the few dazed survivors of his jumble sale.

Cinema

Video Lesbianism
The longest period of time that two women in a pornographic film have sat together on a settee without starting to fondle each other is 8.3 seconds in the 1994 low budget production 'Strap on Sally, Vol. 3' (US).
The longest a woman has sat alone on a settee without starting to fondle herself is 5.2 secs in the same film.

Film Confusion
The greatest length of time a woman has watched a film with her husband without asking a stupid plot-related question was achieved on the 28th October 1990, when Mrs. Ethel Brunswick (GB) sat down with her husband to watch 'The Ipcress File'. She watched in silence for a breathtaking 2 mins 40 secs before asking "Is he a goody or a baddy, then, him in the glasses?", revealing a staggering level of ignorance. This broke her own previous record set in 1962 when she sat through 2 mins 38 secs of "633 Squadron" before asking "Is this a war film, is it?"

Fluffy Toys
The biggest collection of ridiculous fluffy toys on a woman's bed is one of 7046 belonging to 28 year old Sharon Merson (GB) of Bodmin, Cornwall. The collection, weighing 857Kg *1885 lb* includes 2295 teddy bears, 1146 puppies and kittens, 1208 Garfields, 947 Paddingtons, 877 Snoopies and 573 assorted pigs, elephants and gonks -all with their own names! After kissing them all goodnight, a process which takes up to five hours, Miss Merson sleeps on the floor.

Fluffy toys ● Sharon Merson of Cornwall, ready for bed with some of her 7046 fluffy friends.

Banbury, in the strictest confidence, that she was having an affair with the butcher. After Mrs. Blatherwick left at 2.10 pm, Mrs. Banbury immediately began to tell everyone, swearing them all to secrecy. By 2.30pm, she had told 128 people of the news. By 2.50 pm it had risen to 372 and by 4.00 that afternoon, 2774 knew of the affair, including the local Amateur Dramatic Society, several knitting circles, a coachload of American tourists which she flagged down and the butcher's wife. When a tired Mrs. Banbury went to bed at 11.55 that night, Mrs. Blatherwick's affair was common knowledge to a staggering 75,338 people, enough to fill Wembley Stadium.

Gossiping ● Mrs Agnes Banbury of Cheadle, Cheshire. Britain's champion scandal monger.

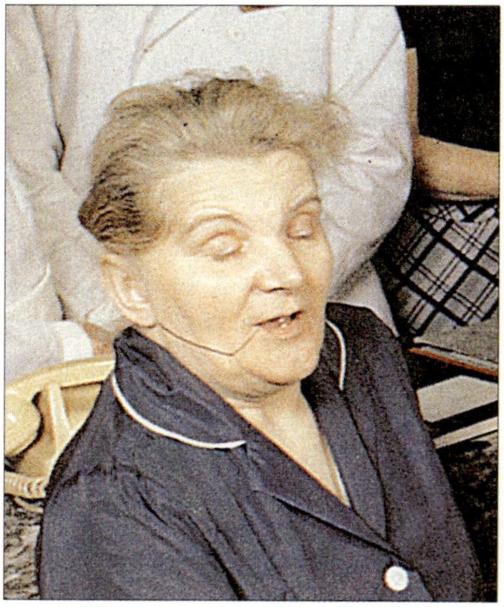

Huff Longevity
The longest recorded huff taken by a woman was one of 57 years 9 months 8 days by Mrs Glenda Bavington (GB). Following a misunderstanding over a sausage roll and an egg sandwich at a New Years Eve party in 1936, she went into a huff with her sister Betty and didn't talk to her again until their father's funeral on 8th October 1994. Despite working alongside each other on the bakery counter of the local Co-op in Aberystwyth, Dyfed for the first forty years of the record, Mrs. Bavington looked straight through her sister and pretended she wasn't there. At a New Years Eve party in 1994, the subject of the sausage roll was brought up again and the huff recommenced, lasting until Betty's death earlier this year.

Miscellaneous

Daytime TV
The greatest amount of Australian soaps watched in a single eight hour day without getting out of the chair was 34 hrs 28 mins by Mrs. Rita Cunliff (GB). This record was achieved using five television sets and three video recorders on 22nd January 1996. When Mrs. Cunliff's husband returned from work he had to make his own tea.

Group Toilet Visit
The record for the largest group of women to visit a toilet simultaneously is held by 147 workers at the Department of Social Security, Longbenton. At their annual Christmas celebration at a nightclub in Newcastle upon Tyne on October 12th 1994, Mrs Beryl Crabtree got up to go to the toilet and was immediately followed by 146 other members of the party. Moving as a mass, the group entered the toilet at 9.52pm and, after waiting for everyone to finish, emerged 2 hrs 37 mins later.

Orangest skin
On March 4th 1995, Miss Kelly Marie Prestwick (GB), a sales assistant in the perfume department of the John Lewis store in Leeds was independently assessed by chromotologists from the Laboratoire Garnier as having a skin orangeness equivalent to 165 on the Pantone classification scale. This is about twice as orange as the skin of a satsuma.

THE SEXIST TIMES

Single Breath Sentence Record SMASHED!

AN Oxfordshire woman today became the first ever to break the thirty minute barrier for talking without drawing breath.

Mrs Mavis Sommers, 48, of Cowley smashed the previous record of 23 minutes when she excitedly reported an argument she'd had in the butchers to her neighbour. She ranted on for a staggering 32 minutes 12 seconds without pausing for air before going blue and collapsing in a heap on the ground. She was taken to the Radcliffe Infirmary in a wheelbarrow but was released later after check-ups.

At the peak of her mammoth motormouth marathon, she acheived an unbelievable 680 words per minute, repeating the main points of the story an amazing 114 times whilst her neighbour, Mrs Dolly Knowles nodded and tutted. The last third of the sentence was delivered in a barely audible croak, the last two minutes being mouthed only, accompanied by vigorous gesticulations and indignant spasms.

October 18th 1996

The World of Men

Food and Drink

Beer Drinking
The greatest amount of beer drunk before going to the lavatory was 25.5 litres *45 pints* of assorted weak lagers by Mr. George Wingfield (GB), downed in various pubs in Knutsford High Street, Cheshire, between 12.15pm and 2.38pm on the 22nd December 1986.

Hottest Curry Eaten
Many claims are made about the ferocity of curries eaten, but in the main they are difficult to substantiate. The hottest verifiable curry eaten was a XXXHot Chicken Murg Thaal with extra chilies consumed by George Wingfield (GB) at the Bengal Tiger Restaurant, Knutsford on 23rd December 1986. The curry was reportedly so hot that between kitchen and table it burst into flames, singeing the waiter's eyebrows.

Beer drinking ● George Wingfield, holder of many of the least enviable records in this book.

Physiology

Urinating
The longest piss delivered at one continuous scoot was one of 36 mins 24 secs by Mr George Wingfield (GB) in the doorway of a newsagents shop in Knutsford High Street on 22nd December 1986. Mr. Wingfield was arrested and charged with a public order offence 17 minutes into his record attempt, but arresting officers had to wait a further 19mins 24 seconds before taking him back to the station for a kicking.

Biggest Fart
The largest and most catastrophic fart was one dropped by Mr. George Wingfield (GB) in the car park of the Dog and Duck, Knutsford on the morning of 24th December 1986. Suffering from terrible guts, Mr. Wingfield gingerly attempted to squeak one out whilst bending to pick up his car keys, but the resulting flatulent explosion blew his entire digestive tract out his arse. Attending firemen hosed down his smoking guts for two hours before paramedics with breathing apparatus could begin the process of pushing them back up.

Expletives

On 9th June 1996, Mr. Harold Brayson (GB) struck his thumb with a stone mason's mallet whilst breaking concrete in his back yard in Tewksbury, Gloucestershire. He went on to swear for 14 mins 7 secs without stopping or once repeating a swear word. He later attempted to better this feat on BBC TV's Record Breakers programme by dropping a car battery on his foot. It ended in failure when he repeated the word bastard after 12 mins 58 secs.

Expletives ● Harold Brayson gets ready to turn the air blue.

Pottest belly

The overhanging beergut belonging to Trevor Chisholme (GB) of Chorley, Lancs weighed in on July 7th 1996 at a mammoth 148.7 kg *23 st 6lb.* Not including his record breaking super pot, Mr. Chisholme himself would weigh a mere 49.3 kg *7 st 10lb.* He achieved this impressive feat in only 8 years of relentless heavy drinking, during which time his trouser waist size has remained the same whilst his pot has ballooned above his belt. Having a bilge tank the size of Mr. Chisholme's would be equivalent to walking around with World Champion shot putter Geoff Capes lying in the bottom of your vest.

Holiday Gymnastics

The greatest number of press-ups done in front of some girls on a beach is 6 by Wayne Fletcher (GB) whilst on holiday in San Antonio, Ibiza on 19th August 1988. The girls went off with a waiter.

Uselessness

The record for the greatest inability to do anything practical is held by Rex Broadbent (GB) of Preston, Lancs. During forty years of marriage, Mr. Broadbent's long suffering wife Freda, cooked, washed, ironed, did all the housework, held down two cleaning jobs and brought up six children while her husband, an unemployed gas fitter, watched the telly. On June 28th 1991, she went into hospital to have a hysterectomy, leaving Rex to fend for himself. However, unaware of where the kitchen was, he died of dehydration after just four days, waiting for his wife to come home and make a cup of tea.

Biggest Hockle

Whilst taking a lunchtime stroll from his local pub to the bookmakers on September 8th 1973, Patrick O'Dougle (GB) 1932-1974, a 180-a-day smoker (untipped) stopped momentarily on a street corner in Tipton, West Midlands, to eructate. The record breaking greb he produced was the size of a fully grown tabby cat and was described by horrified witnesses as looking a bit like black cauliflower cheese.

Biggest hockle ● Patrick O'Dougle, the man who brought up a two gallon prairie oyster.

Starting

Scrapyard owner 'Fighting' Frankie Smith (GB) of Blyth, Northumberland, currently holds all UK starting records. In a 26 year starting career, he has started on no fewer than 35, 577 innocent people, mainly in the pubs

Uselessness ● Rex Broadbent hard at work doing all he was capable of doing.

and clubs of Blyth and Ashington. On December 26th 1991, between 12.30 pm and 11.55 pm, he started on 512 people in the Dog and Hammer public house, the most ever achieved in a single day. Smith also holds the record for the oiliest dog and most unstable pile of crashed cars.

Driving

Loudest Car Stereo

The Saisho stereo fitted in the Mk.II Escort belonging to Wayne Fletcher (GB) reached a momentary peak noise level of 312 dB whilst waiting at traffic lights next to some girls in Stockport, Cheshire on 8th July 1988. This noise level is equivalent to 8 Concordes taking off inside the car. The girls walked off.

Car Customisation

Judged as a proportion of the overall value of the car, the accessories fitted to the MarkII Escort of Wayne Fletcher (GB) add up to the world's most expensive car customisation project at 105761%. Between 8th March 1986 and 22nd September 1996, Fletcher had spent a grand total of £63, 456.99 at the Stockport branch of Halfords in an attempt to attract girls to his vehicle. His fruitless purchases include a Paddy Hopkirk Full Body Styling Kit (£3500), 'Nightrider' style Disco Stop Lights (£199), Split 45 Weber Carburettors x4 (£200), Scorpion Talking Alarm (£500) and a Chromium plated Mock Twin Exhaust Extension (£285). The car is currently valued at £50 to £60.

Longest Wheel Spin

The greatest length of time a car has screeched its wheels to impress some girls was achieved on 9th July 1988 by Wayne Fletcher (GB) in his MarkII Escort. When traffic lights in Stockport, Cheshire turned green, Fletcher attempted to pull off at such speed that his front wheels spun for an amazing 42 secs before the car began to move. Both tyres fell to pieces and the clutch dropped out twenty yards down the road. The girls walked off.

Rep driving ● Mel Henshaw demonstrates his skills as he crosses the central reservation.

Beach gymnastics, loudest car stereo, longest wheel spin ● Wayne Fletcher holder of many showing off records.

Rep Driving

The most impressive display of multi-task driving was achieved by Powdered Egg Salesman Mel Henshaw (GB) at the wheel of his Vauxhall Cavalier 21 GLi. On February 12th 1992, whilst driving at 112 mph in freezing fog on the M1 in South Yorkshire, he simultaneously shaved, ate a sandwich, dictated a letter, read a road map, filled in his expenses, re-tuned the radio, took his jacket off, smoked a cigarette, and spoke to his wife on his mobile phone.

For Whom The Bells Toll
PART TWO
PIZZA SHED
WELL, THANKYOU VERY MUCH FOR THE FLOWERS SIDNEY, AND FOR TAKING ME OUT. I JUST LOVE ITALIAN FOOD.
AYE, ME AN' AALL, PET. 'SPECIALLY THAT CHEESE, Y'KNAA... THE STUFF WHAT HONKS LIKE SPEW.
OOOH! YOU KNOW, I THINK I'VE HAD A BIT TOO MUCH WINE. I'VE NEVER HAD A WHOLE GLASS BEFORE...
... WHAT WITH THAT AND SHERRY TRIFLE... giggle!
heh! heh!
OH, LOOK AT THE TIME, SIDNEY. NEARLY TEN O'CLOCK. I'D BEST BE GETTING HOME OR ELSE DADDY WILL WORRY.
NAAH, LISTEN, PET. WHY DIVVEN'T YU COME BACK TU MY PLACE FORRA CUP O' COFFEE?
BINGO AND STUFF
OH, NO... I DON'T THINK I'D BETTER...
BUT I'VE GOT SUMMAT TU ASK YU. THERE'S SUMMAT I WANT YU T'DEE FORRUZ.
WELL, ASK ME NOW. I MAY BE ABLE TO DO IT RIGHT HERE.
EEH NAAH, PET. I COULDN'T. NOT HERE IN THE STREET.
OH, COME ON THEN, LET'S GO.
SHORTLY...
REET PET. WHAT D'YU WANT T'DRINK?
OOOH. WHAT HAVE YOU GOT?
EVERYTHING...
... ACE ... HARP... CARLING... McEWANS ... BROON ... THE LOT.
ERM... I'LL HAVE ANYTHING, THANKYOU.
THERE YU GAN, PET.
OH, THANKYOU... ... SPECIAL BREW?
AYE...
... ERM... SPECIAL BREW FORRA SPECIAL LADY.
WHERE'S YOUR MUM, SIDNEY? I'M LOOKING FORWARD TO MEETING HER...
ERM... AUSTRALIA. SHE'S OOT VISITIN' RELATIVES. WUZ'VE GOT THE PLACE TU WUSELVES.
MAM'S ROOM
ZZZZ!

SO, WHAT IS IT YOU WANTED TO ASK ME, SIDNEY?
OH, AYE... WELL, ERM... ERM... DRINK UP, PET... ...ERM...WUZ'VE BEEN GANNIN' OOT FORRA WEEK NOO...
YES, SEVEN WONDERFUL DAYS.
...AND... ERM... ERM... ERM...
...YU'VE GOT FUCKIN' LOVELY EYES, PET...
OOH, THANKYOU.
...AND, WELL... I THOUGHT IT'S ABOOT TIME THAT WUZ... I MEAN YOU... SORT OF...
... AN' I LOVE YER HAIR, PET...
FLATTERER... TEE! HEE!
... AND I WUNDAD ... IF Y'D ... SU... Y'KNAA, WOULD Y'PLEASE... SU...
ARE YOU TRYING TO ASK WHAT I THINK YOU'RE TRYING TO ASK?
AYE!! I AM PET. I AM.
OH, I'VE BEEN WAITING FOR YOU TO ASK ME!
WHAT?... SUR... Y'WILL LIKE?
YES! YES! OF COURSE I WILL, SIDNEY!
FUCKIN' MAGIC!
LET'S GO AND ASK MY FATHER RIGHT AWAY.
AYE, PET.
TREMBLE TREMBLE
EH!?!
... ASK YER FATHA!?!... ...WHAT FAWA?
OH, I KNOW IT'S A LITTLE OLD-FASHIONED, BUT I'D LIKE HIS BLESSING BEFORE WE DO IT.
BUT...
ZZZIP!
... AFTER ALL, YOU ONLY DO IT ONCE AND I WANT TO DO IT PROPERLY
WELL... I MEAN... IF YER SURE, LIKE.
YES. COME ON... LET'S GO NOW.

SO, SHORTLY...
HELLO SIDNEY, WE'VE HEARD A LOT ABOUT YOU.
DADDY, SIDNEY HAS SOMETHING TO ASK YOU.
OH? WELL, ASK AWAY, LAD.
ERM... AYE, WELL, ...I... ER... I WUNDAD LIKE... ERM... IF...
...WELL ... I WUNDA IF Y'D LET WENDY ... ERM... SU... SU... IF, LIKE, Y'KNAA, IF IT'S AALREET WI' YEE, IF SHE COULD... ERM...
OUT WITH IT, SIDNEY... OUT WITH IT.
... IF SHE COULD... ER... GIVE US A B... B... B... Y'KNAA... GIVE US A B... B... BL...
I WANT A B... A... B... I WANT A B... B... BL...
OH! THE CAT'S GOT HIS TONGUE...
...HE WANTS TO MARRY ME!
HOW LOVELY! OF COURSE YOU CAN MARRY HER, SIDNEY MY BOY, OF COURSE YOU CAN!
WELCOME TO THE FAMILY...
...SON!
RIGHT! THERE'S NOT A MINUTE TO LOSE.
I'LL PHONE THE VICAR AND BOOK THE CHURCH FOR AUGUST 10th, THEN I'LL CALL THE BAKER AND ORDER A GREAT BIG CAKE. WENDY, YOU ORGANISE YOUR DRESS.
NOW, WENDY. I'VE HIRED A MARQUEE AND ORCHESTRA, AND I'VE MADE A LIST OF ALL THE GUESTS FROM OUR SIDE. HAVE A LOOK THROUGH AND SEE IF I'VE MISSED ANYONE OUT. THEN GIVE IT TO SIDNEY TO SEE IF HE'D LIKE TO ADD A FEW FROM HIS SIDE.
RIGHT, DADDY. I'M JUST GOING TO ORDER MY FLOWERS.
CAKE'S ARRIVING ON TUESDAY, DADDY, AND THE VINTAGE CARS ARE HIRED.

CONTINUED ON PAGE 19

AARON A. AARDVARK

Incompetent Domestic Builder

★DRAINS CRACKED ★ CARPETS RUINED ★ CEMENT MIXED ON YOUR PATIO

All prices include 6 bags of hardened cement left by your front door. Plaster trailed through your home at no extra cost!

TEL: (0191) 233 002

Aaron A. Aardvark - not very good, but first in the book

Have-a-Go Builders

Established 1996

For a complete building service

BRICKWORK? PLASTERING? ROOFING? GLAZING? PLUMBING?

WE'LL HAVE A SHOT AT THE LOT!

ALL WORK UNDERTAKEN BY UNSKILLED BUT ENTHUSIASTIC WORKERS

TEL: 0191 377 353

You've tried the best - now try the rest!

Dodgy Brothers

Dubious Building Services

Time served tradesmen plus a couple of blokes you don't want in your house.

All building work undertaken plus:

- Sex chat lines called in your absence.
- Underwear drawers rifled and lingerie stolen.
- Wife's bra put on head - ***GUARANTEED!***
- Follow up dirty phone calls to your missus.

(0191) 212 001

INVISIBLE BROS.

Tired of waiting in for builders who turn up late? Then call us and go out, because we don't turn up **at all.** No explanations. Nothing.

INVISIBLE BROS. Domestic Builders.

Specialists in:
★ Not turning up

Tel (0191) 469 790

For specialists in unpredictable hours and unexplained absences for weeks on end call

SPORADIC BUILDING SERVICES

We offer a range of services from puncturing the gas main on Christmas Eve to flooding your bathroom with shit and going on holiday for a month

Ask about:

- **JOBS LEFT HALF FINISHED**
- **CARS BLOCKED IN BY SKIPS FOR WEEKS ON END**
- **UNTILED ROOFS POLYTHENED OVER THROUGHOUT WINTER**
- **WILDLY OPTIMISTIC ESTIMATES OF HOW LONG IT WILL TAKE**

Slight drizzle? NO PROBLEM. We're off home.

For unreliable service at imaginative prices ring

0191 377 353

SEXIST BUILDERS LTD. Est. 1952

Complete Domestic Harrassment Specialists

*WOLF WHISTLES *SUGGESTIVE COMMENTS *LEERING *OPTIMISTIC PASSES AT HOUSEWIVES *SWEARING *OBSCENE GESTURES

FEDERATION OF SWEATY-ARSED BUILDERS

A company with 44 years in the trade. Our craftsmen have Dagenham Smiles second to none and use only the foulest language in front of your children and neighbours

Call (0191) 416 790

RELUCTANT REPAIRS

Building & Roofing Repairs
All jobs too large or too small

Call now for a fuck off price

Tel (0191) 377 353
(ansaphone)

Buffalo Billding Services,
104 Shit Street .... Tyneside 0191 233 002

ROBDOG & SON

Overpriced Property Repair Service

Give us a call and kiss your savings goodbye.

The price we say is the price you pay - *and the fucking rest*

Tel. (0191) 377 353

Two Hoots Contractors

Boorish, ill-manered builders.

- *Prompt, efficient service*
- *Gardens laid waste by boots*
- *Gallons of your tea demanded*
- *Very loud Radio One all day*
- *Polite requests acknowledged and completely ignored*

Tel. (0191) 284 349

Remember- we ALWAYS pay the scantest regard to your property

Jack Churchill & Son

A name you can trust - that's why I picked it.

For all your discouraging behaviour requirements.

Specialists in

★ TUTTING ★ SIGHING
★ PUSHING BACK HAT
★ SCRATCHING HEAD
★ SUCKING TEETH ★ WINCING

Tel. (0191) 233 002

NOT IN BUILDERS

For extensions, dormer windows, loft conversions - don't call us now, we're not in.

Tel. (0191) 212001

Sweaty Arsed Builders,
102 Hairy Knacker Street....0191 377 353

WHO DID THAT? BUILDERS

SPECIALISTS IN CRITICISING PREVIOUS BUILDING WORK

✻ ***Others builders slagged off***
✻ ***Your D.I.Y. laughed at***
✻ ***Over reaction guaranteed***

We're also experts in prognostications of doom

Tel. 0191 284 349

Ne'er Do Well Builders,
103 Hairy Knacker Street....0191 377 353

Served Time Tradesmen Ltd.

The local builders you really can't trust

Specialists in

★ Stealing your lead flashing
★ Mysterious and arbitrary additional pricing systems
★ Things going missing

Call: (0191) 212 001

All quotations are likely to change depending on how much we think we can get from you. Fantastic prices for OAP's living alone.

For service with a 'Nile' it's got to be...

Wilson, Kepple & Betty

Traditional Egyptian builders Est. 4000BC

For a full service in sphinx and pyramid erection. No job too colossal.

- HIEROGLYPHIC PLANS DRAWN UP
- LABOURERS ENTOMBED
- CURSES BESTOWED

Call us now and we'll be round in the morning with 10,000 slaves to give you an estimate.

*From papyrus to topping out in six generations or your money back - **no quibbles.***

Call Tyneside (0191) 284 349
and ask for Amenhotep III

BARELY-ADEQUATE LTD.

Reasonable quality building work but nothing to sing about.

Tel. (0191) 284 349

You Get What You Pay For With

KOST KUT KONSTRUCTORS

Specialists in all domestic building work done on the cheap.

All work done comes with our 25 year worthless guarantee

Brickwork-Joinery-Plumbing-Roofing
Building regulations? - *fuck 'em
***Poor quality materials used**
***All responsibilities shirked**

We have NO INSURANCE OVERHEADS!

Ring (0191) 233 002

We work to a price, not to a standard

ADVERTISEMENT

THE INSULT THAT MADE A SEXIST OUT OF "CEDRIC"

Sidney Smutt

Awarded the title "The World's Most Sexist Man"

Let Me PROVE I Can Make YOU a SEXIST!

ARE you "fed up" with overweight, beer swilling animals getting all the laughs in the pub by lighting farts and doing "last turkey in the shop"? Sick and tired of having to go to the toilet for a wee after a puny six or seven pints, when we all know that the top shelf tarts won't drop 'em for any man who can't swallow at least a gallon before straining his potatoes? I know just how you feel because, believe it or not, I used to be HALF A MAN too!

My Secret

Then I discovered a wonderful way to develop sexism fast. It worked wonders for me - changed me from a polite ten stone nobody who never got a sniff of kipper to a sweaty fourteen stone brass-necked gob-shite who has to beat back the high end skirt (who swallow) with a shitty stick.

My patented five point plan involves 300 minutes a day of pleasant practice in the privacy of your room or shed. My method involves no weights, pulleys or springs, just simple things you already have in the home: 120 Embassy Regal, 36 large cans of lager, a boil-in-the-bag curry and the Freemans catalogue. This method has already helped thousands of other fellows become bloated mindless wankers like me in double quick time.

I will make you a Sexist FAST

If you're like I was, you'll want a galvanised kebab proof digestive system and mindless-ly offensive personality you can be proud of anytime. You'll want the Jocky Wilson type physique and flatulent personal magnetism that women rave about at the beach or pub. The kind that makes other fellows green with envy.

SIDNEY SMUTT,
Institute of Sexism, Scrogg Road, Walker

Dear Sid, I am interested in developing the following qualities:

- [ ] Overhanging bilge tank you can rest a pint on
- [ ] Inflammable trench warfare type gasses from all orifices
- [ ] Minimum ten pint bladder capacity
- [ ] Ability to half remember a number of old Bernard Manning jokes
- [ ] Pallid, rhubarb-like complexion
- [ ] Rounded shoulders and stooping gait
- [ ] Hacking phlegmy cough
- [ ] Hugely enlarged swearing vocabulary
- [ ] Hugely reduced non-swearing vocabulary

Name.................................... Address....................................

....

I accept that the Sidney Smutt method may involve a small but significant risk of cancer (bowel/lung), degenerative liver disease, stunted growth, hairy palms and going blind, a hefty fine and/or imprisonment.

For Whom The Bells Toll
PART THREE
NEXT EVENING...
YER GERRIN' FUCKIN' WHAAT?!
MARRIED, BOB MAN... I'M GERRIN' FUCKIN' MARRIED... AN' THERE'S NAE ESCAPE... IT'S AAL ARRANGED!
WELL HOW THE FUCK DID THAT HAPPEN?
I FOLLOWED YOUR FUCKIN' ADVICE, BAZ, THAT'S HOW IT FUCKIN' HAPPENED...
...AN' BY THE WAY, YE OWE US A BLUR JOB.
WELL YU MUST'VE DONE SUMMIK WRANG, SID... WHAT DID YU DEE?
WHY, I DIVVEN'T KNAA. I THOUGHT I'D ASKED 'ER T' SUCK US OFF, LIKE...
...NEXT THING I KNAA I'M BEING FITTED FORRA FUCKIN' CLAW HAMMER COAT.
I CANNAT GET MARRIED. I HAVEN'T SURRED ME WILD URRTS YET.
EH?
EH?
ER... I MEAN... I HAVEN'T FINISHED SURRIN' THEM YET.
WELL, WHAT ARE Y'GANNIN' T'DEE, SID? Y'VE GOT T' DEE SUMMAT.
THERE'S URNLY ONE THING TU DEE...
...I'M GANNIN' T'JOIN THE FRENCH FOREIGN LEGION!
DIVVUN' TAALK YER FUCKIN' SHITE, MAN. THERE'S NAE NEED T'GAN THAT FAR. WUZ'RE FOUR INTELLIGENT BLURKS... WELL... THREE OF US AN' JOE... AN' IF WE PUT W'HEEDS TOGETHER, WUZ CAN HAVE IT SORTED OOT IN NAE TIME.
AYE, YER REET THERE, LET'S GET THINKIN'.
AYE.
11·30pm...
LA LA LA-LA LAAAA... DE DE DEEE LA-LA LAAA...
HOWAY, YEEZ LOT... ...OOT!
THE FOX & HOOND
HOWAY, LET'S GAN CLUBBIN' AT RITZY'S.
AYE. SUNDER NEET'S FANNY NEET AT RITZY'S.
PUBLIC BAR
AYE... AALREET... ERM... BUT...
BUT WHAT, SID MAN?
IT'S JUST... ERM... ERM...
YOO-HOO!!...
...SIDNEY!...

...SORRY I'M LATE, SIDNEY, ONLY THE PRAYER MEETING WENT ON A BIT. ANYWAY, I'M LOOKING FORWARD TO THE NIGHTCLUB...
PUBLIC BAR
...ONLY SOFT DRINKS FOR YOU, THOUGH SIDNEY... YOU'VE GOT TO BE UP EARLY TOMORROW. WE'RE GOING TO CHOOSE THE ENGAGEMENT RINGS, REMEMBER?
SHORTLY...
...BLAH! BLAH! BLAH!...SO YOUR SIDE IS HAVING YELLOW CARNATIONS AND MY SIDE WHITE LILLIES, WHAT DO YOU THINK? AND REMIND ME TO ORDER THE CORSAGE AND CAN YOU CUT A FEW GUESTS FROM YOUR SIDE, ONLY THERE'S FAR TOO MANY...
RITZY'S
Ritzy's NITE SPOT
INSIDE...
......BUT I JUST CAN'T DECIDE BETWEEN IVORY WITH THE SCALLOPED EDGE AND OLD ENGLISH SCRIPT OR THE PLAIN OFF-WHITE WITH THE CRINKLED EDGE AND THE SILVER SERIF TYPE, MUMMY LIKES IVORY BUT I'M NOT SURE AND WHAT ABOUT THE CAKE, MUMMY SAYS WE MUST HAVE PILLARS ON THE CAKE, IT'S NOT A PROPER WEDDING UNLESS THERE'S PILLARS ON THE CAKE, SO MUMMY SAYS HOW MANY PILLARS DO YOU WANT, SIDNEY, HOW MANY PILLARS DO YOU WANT, SIDNEY? PILLARS PILLARS HOW MANY PILLARS, SIDNEY, PILLARS SIDNEY, PILLARS, HOW MANY...?
ERM... ERM...
...WELL YOU THINK ABOUT IT. I'M OFF TO THE LITTLE LADIES ROOM TO POWDER MY NOSE.
WAIT HERE FOR ME.
HI, THERE...
...I'VE BEEN WATCHING YOU. YOU'RE MY KIND OF GUY. FANCY COMING BACK TO MY PLACE FOR A NIGHT OF THE WILDEST SEX YOU'VE EVER HAD?
GUMPH!
OH, DEAR! LOOKS LIKE I'M TOO LATE. I FANCIED GETTING MY DIRTY HANDS ON HIM.
NOT TO WORRY. YOU COME BACK TO MY PLACE AS WELL...I THINK THERE'S ENOUGH OF HIM TO GO ROUND... AND I'VE GOT A VERY BIG BED.

CAN I COME TOO? I'M AS HORNY AS HELL,...WE COULD ALL STRIP DOWN TO OUR UNDERWEAR AND HAVE A LESBIAN CAT-FIGHT OVER HIM WHILE HE WATCHES.

WELL, SIDNEY, WHAT DO YOU THINK? HOW MANY DO YOU WANT?
AALL OF 'EM!...
I'LL HAVE AALL THREE OF 'EM!

OOH, YOU'VE GOT TO HAVE MORE THAN THREE PILLARS ON A CAKE, SIDNEY, YOU NEED AT LEAST FOUR ON EACH TIER, OTHERWISE IT'S UNSTABLE MUMMY SAYS...

CONTINUED ON PAGE 26

Fulchester Joint Matriculation Board

GCE Ordinary Level Examination Paper

Sexism Studies

A stiflingly hot afternoon, June, 1980
time allowed 3 hrs

Attempt all questions. If you do not know the answer to a particular question, attempt to look at someone else's paper by knocking your biro onto the floor and having a shufty while you lean over to retrieve it. You are allowed one visit to the toilet to look at the answers you wrote on the wall yesterday. After ten minutes, request more paper to shit up the other candidates into thinking that you must have wrote loads. Attempt to introduce the one or two facts you are reasonably sure of into the answers to every question. At 4.30 exactly, everybody cough to make the invigilator jump. With three minutes to go, suddenly realise there are 4 more questions on the back of the page that you haven't spotted. You are going to fail.

Section A (20%)

1. Explain why the best women's football team in the world wouldn't stand a chance against you and ten of your mates. Include in your answer
   a) why they are unable to kick a ball straight
   b) what you wouldn't mind doing with them in the bath after the match, though.

2. Pamela Anderson's tits are plastic but look good in photographs. Compare and contrast the relative merits of plastic and real tits for recreational purposes.

3. It is a long established fact that fat lasses are more grateful for it. Outline some of the reasons why this is so, and explain why all feminists are fat, ugly lesbians.

4. Write a critique of any ONE of the following films you will have watched at your mates house while his parents were away for the weekend.
   a) Sex Boat
   b) Three Into One Will Go
   c) King Dong
   d) Speared by Zulu Lovers

5. Women drivers, eh? Discuss.

Section B (20%)

1. Describe an experiment to impress a girl by lighting a fart. What apparatus would you require? What risks would you run in lighting a fart and what are the benefits? Write a balanced chemical equation to describe the reaction that takes place when an eggy fart is lit in a pub with a match.

2. Explain, using diagrams if necessary, how it is possible to tell if a woman is a virgin or not from the way she walks.

3. Name something a woman has invented.

4. Argue heatedly over the respective merits of the Lambourghinni Diablo and the Ferrari Testerossa without ever having seen, let alone driven, either.

5. On average, women live 7 years longer than men yet get their pension 5 years earlier. Explain why this isn't fair, making reference to your lazy old granny who lived to be 100 and your poor grandad who worked 52 years down the pit and died the day before he retired.

ON SALE NOW!

North East

Wife Trader

1st December -7th December ON SALE AT NEWSAGENTS FROM THURSDAY *Price £1* (£50 from printers on Wednesday)

The Regions No.1 Best Selling Wife Mart!!

LOOKING FOR A WIFE?

1000's OF LOCAL SPOUSE BARGAINS EACH WEEK!!

WIFE UNDER £100? ADVERTISE IN THIS SECTION

WITH A PHOTO **Only £5** FOR 1 WEEK

MRS. SIMPKINS, 1942 two tone brunette and grey, 18.2 stone, bodywork needs tidying, good solid reliable wife, super cook, tinted glasses, reluctant sale, first to see will buy, only £3.50 ono. Tel. XXXX XXXXXX

MRS. COLLIS, 1922 classic wife, maintained regardless of cost, bills for £100's, mint condition, new hips in 1986, since used only for shopping, eats like a mouse, £300 may p/ex for busty goer with suspenders. Tel. XXXX XXXXXX

OVER **3150** EXECUTIVE & PRESTIGE WIVES

MRS. LLOYD-JONES, 1950 top of range wife, managing directors missus since new, immaculately maintained inside and out, face professionally rebuilt six months ago, slight drinking problem, looks £1000, only £40. Gold digging secretary forces sale. Tel. XXXX

MRS. PEMBERTON, 1938 small economical runabout wife, curly hair, six months WI membership, 12 months bowls club, two careful husbands, leather handbag, stylish sun glasses, re-offered due to time waster. £25 no offers. Tel. XXXX XXXXXX

MRS. GOLIGHTLY, 1902 fishwife, married last 60 years, tax exempt, nags smashing, still in original hat, some teeth, very rare in this condition, scowls first time, comes with 14 cats and B/W television. Outstanding bargain £30. Tel XXXX XXXXXX

OVER **750** VINTAGE COLLECTORS WIVES

MRS. ANDERSON, 1962 36DD sporty wife, blonde, topless in summer, eyecatching bodywork, long legs, goes like a rabbit, a real head turner. £400, reluctant sale due to affair with milkman. Tel. XXXX XXXXXX

MRS. TALBOT, 1934 grey hair, new teeth, recently replaced glasses, full medical history, knits smashing, good condition for year, any inspection welcome, bargain at only £20. Tel. XXXX XXXXXX

IMMEDIATE RESPONSE!!

Mr. Talbot of Shiremoor was very happy after he sold his wife on the first day of publication to a buyer who travelled from Harrogate. He said "I'd been trying to get shot of her for ages without any sucess. Thank you Wife Trader!"

OVER **1500** PIGS AND HOUNDS

WHO IS THAT MASKED MAN SOARING HIGH ABOVE BIGTOWN CITY LIKE AN EAGLE OF JUSTICE? HALF A NATION THRILLS TO HIS HEROIC EXPLOITS. HIS NAME IS A GOLDEN SYMBOL OF HOPE TO DOWNTRODDEN MEN AND A MIGHTY THORN IN THE SIDE OF FEMINISTS EVERYWHERE! HE IS...
CAPTAIN SEXIST
WELL, JUST ANOTHER QUIET DAY IN BIGTOWN CITY. NO SIGN OF ANY FEMINIST ACTIVITY.
OH-OH! WHAT'S THIS? I THINK I SPOKE TOO SOON!
...I'M VERY SORRY MS. HODGSON, BUT I WAS UP WATCHING THE PORN AND DRINKING TILL THREE IN THE MORNING. I OVERSLEPT AND MISSED MY BUS...
THAT'S NO EXCUSE, ROBINSON.
THIS IS THE THIRD TIME THIS WEEK AND I'M NOT STANDING FOR IT!
HMM. JUST AS I THOUGHT...
A BIRD WITH IDEAS ABOVE HER STATION. TIME TO RIGHT SOME WRONGS!
YOU'RE FINISHED HERE ROBINSON. YOU'VE HAD WRITTEN WARNINGS AND IGNORED THEM. THERE'S NO PLACE FOR YOU IN MY COMPANY. I'M GOING TO WRITE YOUR P45!
BUT MS. HODGSON - I'VE GOT COMMITMENTS. A SEASON TICKET TO UNITED, ACCOUNTS AT THE OFF-LICENCE AND BOOKIES, MY ADULT CHANNEL SUBSCRIPTION.
...NOT TO MENTION THE WIFE AND KIDS.
WA-HAY! ANY CHANCE OF A CUP OF TEA, LOVE? MILK AND SIX SUGARS.
SLAP!
CAPTAIN SEXIST!
'ERE. YOU'VE PUT ON A BIT OF WEIGHT, HAVEN'T YOU? YOU'RE GETTING A BIT OF A DOUBLE CHIN.
GASP!
MIND YOU, THAT'S A NICE DRESS. THERE'S A BLOKE SELLING 'EM ON THE MARKET. MILLIONS OF THEM HE'S GOT. A FIVER EACH. I BOUGHT ONE FOR ME GRANNY.
JANICE! BOOK ME IN AT WEIGHTWATCHERS...
..AND HAVE HARRODS SEND SOME DESIGNER DRESSES ROUND.
...ERM... ERM... WHAT WAS I DOING?
YOU WERE GIVING ROBINSON A RISE. DOUBLING HIS WAGES YOU WERE.
...ERM... WAS I? OKAY... ERM... BACK TO YOUR OFFICE THEN ROBINSON.
JANICE, GET ME A FULL-LENGTH MIRROR AND SOME SCALES. AND HAVE THOSE DRESSES ARRIVED..?
GEE! THANKS CAPTAIN SEXIST!
RISE
NO TIME FOR THANKS WHILE MEN ARE STILL LANGUISHING UNDER THE IRON THUMB OF FEMINISM!

For Whom The Bells Toll
PART FOUR
SUR, BAZ... TELL US AGAIN, WHY AM I DRESSED AS A LASS?
AALREET JOE, HERE WE GAN...
...IN TWO MINUTES TIME, SID'S WENDY IS GUNNA WAALK THROUGH THE DOOR FO' TU MEET SID. WHEN SHE DOES, SHE'S GUNNA CATCH 'IM SNOGGIN' WI' ANOTHER LASS... ...YEE!
SHE TEKS A JEALOUS RADGE AN' CAALLS THE WEDDIN' OFF... SID'S PROBLEMS SOLVED.
BUT WHY COULDN'T WUZ GET A PROPER LASS?
I'VE TELT YUZ. WU COULDN'T FIND ONE WHAT WAS PREPARED TU SNOG SID, LIKE.
ME SISTER WOULD'VE DONE IT.
YOUR SISTER LOOKS LESS LIKE A FUCKIN' LASS THAN YEE DEE, JOE MAN.
I'LL SECOND THAT. SHE'S A FUCKIN' PIG, JOE.
WELL, I STILL DIVVEN'T SEE WHY IT HAD T'BE ME WHAT DRESSED UP.
WELL, IT'S SIMPLY 'COZ YOU'RE THE FUCKIN' THICKEST OOT THE LOT O' WUZ.
AYE. I SUPPURZ.
ANYWAYS, JUST REMEMBER: SNOG SID WHEN SHE COMES IN...
YU DID TELL 'ER EIGHT O'CLOCK, DIDN'T YU, SID?
AYE. EIGHT O'CLOCK.
OKAY JOE! HERE SHE IS.
SNOG! SNOG! SLURP!
MMMMPH!
?

SLURP! SNOG!
SLURP! SLURP! SNOG!
TUT! EIGHT O'CLOCK, HE SAID...
IT'S AALLREET JOE, MAN. Y'CAN STOP NOO... SHE'S WENT.
DID SHE SEE 'IM, THEN, EH?
DID SHE FUCK, JOE.
SHE JUST SEEN THE BACK O'YOUR HEED, Y' FUCKIN BIG TWAT!
GASP! GASP! GASP! GASP!
I'LL GAN AN' FETCH HER BACK. THIS TIME SID GANS ON TOP.
NAH! GASP! - I'D RATHER MARRY HER THAN HAVE HIS TONGUE DOON ME FUCKIN' THRURT AGAIN!
WHOSE ROOND IS IT?
HAD ON A MINUTE. SHE SAID... IF SHE SEEN YU LOOK AT ANOTHER LASS, THE WEDDIN' WOULD BE OFF!
AYE... SO?
WELL, ME SISTER SAID SHE'D NOT SNOG 'IM FOR AALL THE MONEY IN THE WORLD, BUT I BET SHE'D BE SEEN W' 'IM... FOR ABOOT TWENTY POOND.
GAN ON, BOB.
SO SID AN' HOR WAALK PAST WENDY'S HOOSE. WENDY SEES 'EM BURTH. THE WEDDIN'S OFF. PROBLEM SOLVED.
AYE... BUT WHAT IF SHE'S NOT IN?
AYE... ERM...
...I KNAA. HER FATHA'S GOT A SHOP IN BYKER, HASN'T HE? THEY WAALK PAST THAT INSTEAD. HE SEES 'EM, COMES OOT AN' POPS SID ONE.
TELLS 'IM HE CANNAT MARRY HIS DAUGHTER, AN' NEVER T'DARKEN HIS DOORSTEP AGAIN. COSTS SID A COUPLE O' TEETH, LIKE, BUT HE'S OOT THE FUCKIN' PICKLE.
I'LL DRINK T'THAT, BOB.
ME AN' AALL.
GREAT. YOUR ROOND, SID.

NEXT DAY...
HOW! WHERE'S ME TWENTY POOND, WOR BOB?
HAYSTACKS HAMMERS
SALE ALL PLENISHERS REDUCED
ALL SLEDGES HALF PRICE
OPEN
THERE YU GAN. NOW PUT YER ARM ROOND SID AN' WAALK PAST THAT HAMMA SHOP.
PUT ME ARM ROOND 'IM? Y'NEVER SAID OWT ABOOT THAT. IT'S AN EXTRA TENNER T'PUT ME ARM ROOND 'IM.
£10
FUCKIN' HELL. IT'S A MAN'S LIFE AT STAKE HERE, BOBETTE, WOMAN... JESUS!... I'LL GIVE IT T'YU WHEN WE GET BACK YEM.
SO...
HAYSTACK'S HAMMERS
ALL SLEDGES HALF PRICE
OPEN
EH?! THAT'S SIDNEY!
"KING SLEDGE"
CLAW & BALL
PIN & LUMP
HAYSTACKS HAMMERS
SALE
OY!! SIDNEY!

CONTINUED ON PAGE 33

ROLL UP, ROLL UP, FOR THE MOST SEXIST SHOW ON EARTH
BILLY SMUTT'S CIRCUS
BERT TWO RIVERS
Red Indian Dinner Thrower
Hold your breath as he comes in from the pub and throws his burnt dinner at his wife.
PRINCESS MARINA
Tightrope Walker
Look up and gasp as she treads the high wire 50 feet above the ring- without the aid of knickers!
FEARLESS FREDA
Lady Spider Tamer
You'll not believe your eyes as she takes quite a big spider out the bath- armed only with a glass and a birthday card
OLAF THE FEARLESS
Lion tamer
Shows no fear as he puts his wife's head into a lion's
The World Famous

They're rude, they're crude and
they're been drinking since breakfast
ALFREDO GAZPACCI
Scooter Stuntman
Thrill as he rides blindfold round the ring pinching 60 birds on the arse
STROMBOLI the MIGHTY
Gets the lid off the tomato sauce for his wife- without using the doorframe
THE AMAZING KEITH
Traditional Plate Washing Act
Gasp as Keith's missus washes 40 plates simultaneously- while he has a cup of tea
Plus the
BILLY SMUTT BIG TOP SHOWGIRLS
They can't sing, they can't dance, but they've got massive tits.
APPEARING ALL THIS WEEK AT:
A FIELD KNEE DEEP IN MUD AND ELEPHANT SHIT

Watch for the NIPPLEPRINT envelope dropping through *your* letterbox...

...and get to it before the missus.

Tired of 36 jumbo glossy prints of your glossy jumbo missus smearing herself with sun oil? Fed up with framed enlargements of your wife's enlarged frame? Send your film to us, and we guarantee you'll recieve the **wrong photos.** Completely 'by accident' we'll send you 36 assorted pics of the most gorgeous bird you've ever seen, baking herself on a naturist beach in Spain- and your missus will be none the wiser.

"My wife blew her top when our snaps came back. I told her I would throw them away but I've hid them behind some tins of paint in the garage. Thank you, NipplePrint."

Mr. R.
London

"A thousand thanks for 'mislaying' my photos. My wife is no oil painting, unlike the cracking piece in the topless prints that dropped onto my mat. I told her there must have been a mix up at the labs and the daft cow fell for it."

Mr. B
Essex

Alternatively...

Have you taken a snap of your old boot but managed to get some topless stunner in the background, frolicking in the pool? Throw away your magnifying glass and ask about our Mucky Selective Enlargement Service.

For Whom The Bells Toll
PART FIVE
FRIDAY AFTERNOON...
THE FOX AND HOOND
PUBLIC BAR
FUCK ME, LADS... I'M FINISHED.
THIS TIME THE MORRO' I'LL BE MR. WENDY FUCKIN' HAYSTACKS... NEXT STOP THE PRAM SHOP, THEN IT'S DOONHILL TU THE CREMATORIUM VIA THE FUCKIN' GARDEN CENTRE.
CHEER UP, MAN. WUZ'VE STILL GOT YER STAG NEET TU GAN. WE'LL SEND YEE OOT WI' A BANG AT THE UNION CLUB.
AYE. WE'RE GANNIN' TU SEE THAT COMEDIAN BLURK, CHUBBY ARSE...
... AN' EIGHT STRIPPAZ FROM NOTTINGHAM.
AYE... I SEEN THEM AT SOOTH SHIELDS. CLASS ACT, SID. FIRE BANANAS OOT THEIR TWATS THE' DEE.
AYE. THEN THEY SHAG AALL THE AUDIENCE ON STAGE IN THE SECOND HALF.
ME AN' ME DAD WENT UP LAST TIME.
SUR C'MON, SID MAN, SUP UP, GAN YEM AN' PUT SOME CLEAN UNDAKEX ON. WUZ'LL SEE YU THERE AT SIX.
6.00 pm...
UNION CLUB
NUFC
ACAB
TONITE CHUBBY ARSE + STRIPPERS
PARSNIPS ENGINEERING
HERE HE COMES, LADS. THE CONDEMNED MAN, ABOOT TU SHAG A HEARTY STRIPPER!
AALL REET, LADS? STAG DO, IS IT?
AYE... THIS UN.
POOR CUNT.
... LISTEN, SIT HIM AT THE FRONT, THEN WHEN THE SHAGGIN' STARTS HE'LL BE FOG UP.
REET. THANKS, PAL.
YANK!

ON JUNE 8TH THERE'S GOING TO BE AN ELECTION

Keith Tinsdale, candidate for the Married Man's Party wants your vote.

Alone amongst Britain's major political parties, the MMP recognises that married men are the victims of unfair treatment. Many men work long hours each day, leaving the house early in the morning and often not returning from the pub until gone midnight. On Saturdays they are expected to trudge endlessly round the shops with their wives, buying food and children's clothes when they should be asleep in front of the telly watching football. And thanks to xxxx this government'srelaxation of trading laws, Sundays are no longer a day of rest to be spent in the club, many men being forced to visit garden centres to buy bedding plants. In addition, many married men face the prospect of years of being nagged regularly to put a shelf up. The Married Man's Party believe that change is long overdue and we ask xxxx that on June 8th you help bring about that change.

We in the Married Man's Party DEMAND:

* Our tea on the bloody table when we get in
* How's Your Father on request
* Stop going on all the bloody time
* An end to being asked what the last thing you xxxx said was
* Stop going through our bloody pockets
* Spend as long as we like on the toilet, if neccessary all the way through Exchange and Mart

And we will NOT:

* Change shitty nappies
* Look up from our newspaper at breakfast
* Listen to a single bloody word you say
* Lift a finger in the kitchen
* Lift the toilet seat up before, or down after a Jimmy Riddle
* Have your mother round at Christmas, sticking her bloody nose in

In return we WILL:

* Put spiders outside
* Open sauce bottles
* Put that shelf up. Soon.

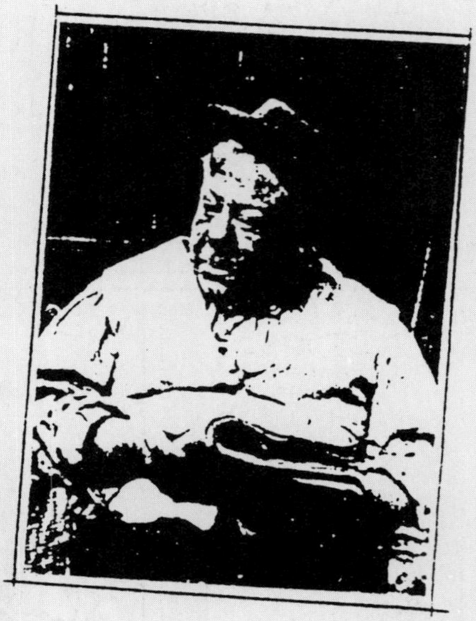

Your Candidate
Keith Tinsdale is a 48 year old panel beater who has lived in the Fulchester East ward all his life. He is largely self educated, but sometimes attended the Councillor Tonks Comprehensive School where he excelled at metalwork and fighting. He is married with 8 or 9 children who all attend local schools and borstals. His xxxx wife Marie is just a housewife. He has a wide range of hobbies, as diverse as drinking, smoking and darts. He can be contacted by his constituents at any time in the snug of the Dog and Hammer, where he holds forth on a number of subjects.

Remember, keep the missus in on June 8th and Vote Married Man

TINSDALE X

COME ON SIDNEY, WE'LL BE LATE.
HOLD ON, HOLD ON... WHAT THE FUCK'S GANNIN' ON HERE, LIKE?
EH?
DON'T TELL ME YOU'VE FORGOTTEN THE WEDDING REHERSAL THIS EVENING, SIDNEY.
AW, HOWAY PET! IT'S EEZ STAG NEET, F' FUCK'S SAKE, MAN.
STAG NIGHT!?! MY SIDNEY'S NOT INTERESTED IN THAT SORT OF THING ANYMORE... ARE YOU, SIDNEY?...
... ARE YOU, SIDNEY?..
...SIDNEY!?
no, Wendy dear...
AW, FUCK IT. WUZ'RE PISSIN' UP THE WAALL HERE. LET'S GAN IN AN SEE CHUBBY ARSE AN' THE STRIPPERS.
NOW, SIDNEY. I'VE CHANGED THE HYMN FROM "JESU, JOY OF MAN'S DESIRING" TO "LOVE DIVINE", BECAUSE I THINK THAT SUMS UP WHAT WE FEEL ABOUT EACH OTHER, DOESN'T IT, SIDNEY?
...AND MUMMY CAN'T DECIDE BETWEEN POTATO SALAD OR COLESLAW IN THE BUFFET, WHAT DO YOU THINK, SIDNEY? AND I'VE SHAVED A FEW MORE GUESTS OFF YOUR SIDE BECAUSE THERE WAS FAR TOO MANY AND DADDY IS PAYING AFTER ALL, SO THERE'S JUST YOUR MUM COMING...
UNION CLUB
...BUT JUST TO THE CHURCH, NOT THE RECEPTION.
SHORTLY...
...10 x 8'S WOULD LOOK NICER THAN 11 x 9'S. BUT THEN 11 x 9'S WOULD LOOK NICE WITHOUT A BORDER, WHAT DO YOU THINK, SIDNEY, AND SHOULD WE HAVE MATT OR GLOSS?
AH, WENDY...SIDNEY...
...WELCOME!
DO COME IN. IT'S LOVELY TO SEE YOU AT THE REHERSAL SIDNEY...
...ONLY I MISSED MINE, SIDNEY, I WAS ON MY STAG DO, HAD CARNAL KNOWLEDGE OF SIX STRIPPERS ON STAGE, I DID... SHAGGED THEIR ARSES OFF...
...OH MY LORD!

SO...
RIGHT, LET'S GET STARTED, SHALL WE?...
SIDNEY, YOU STAND THERE...WENDY YOU STAND THERE. THEN I SAY... "DEARLY BELOVED, WE ARE HERE TODAY IN THE SIGHT OF GOD TO...
...SHIT ON MY WIFE'S TITS, LADIES AND GENTLEMEN...
...SHE SAYS, "YOU DIRTY CUNT. CHUBBY. WHY DON'T YOU JUST...
HAR! HAR! HAR! HAR! HAR!
HAR! HAR! HAR!
... PROMISE TO LOVE, HONOUR AND OBEY, AND WILL YOU, SIDNEY, TAKE WENDY...
...UP THE FUCKIN' ARSE!!
HAR! HAR! HAR!
HAR! HAR! HAR!
...ANYWAYS, I WAS FUCKIN' THE MISSUS LAST NIGHT, AN' SHE SAYS, "CHUBBY, I WISH YOU'D...
... SLIP YOUR FINGER INTO MY RING.
THAT'S IT. THEN I ASK IF ANY MAN KNOWS OF ANY REASON WHY YOU MAY NOT BE MARRIED, LET HIM SPEAK NOW, OR FOREVER HOLD HIS...
...FOUR FOOT COCK.!!
THANK YOU. YOU'VE BEEN A LOVELY AUDIENCE, I'LL FUCK OFF NOW AND LET THE STRIPPERS ON.
HAR! HAR! HAR! HAR!
WELL, SIDNEY, IT'S CUSTOMARY AT THIS POINT TO KISS THE BRIDE.
OH, NO! THERE'LL BE NONE OF THOSE SORTS OF GOINGS ON, WILL THERE, SIDNEY?
RIGHT THEN LADS, WHO'S FIRST UP?
WELL, THAT'S THE REHERSAL OVER, BOTH OF YOU. TOMORROW WILL BE THE REAL THING.

NEXT DAY...
I CANNAT GAN AHEED WITH IT, BAZ... YUV GORRA GERRUZ OOT O'THIS. YEE GORRUZ INTO IT, YEE GERRUZ OOT!
I'M THINKIN', I'M THINKIN' PLENTY O' TIME, SID.
SHE MIGHT NOT TORN UP.
SHE FUCKIN' WILL!
SHE MIGHT DIE IN A CAR CRASH ON THE WAY HERE. LOOK ON THE BRIGHT SIDE, SID.
LAAA...DAAA...DA DEE DA...DAA DAA DUM DA-DA DEE DA DUM
FUCK! SHE'S HERE, BAZ...
QUICK, SID, GET ON THE FLOOR.
EH? WHAT FOR?
LIKE YUV FAINTED.
OH, GOOD IDEA, BAZ. I CAN LIE THERE FOR THE REST O' ME FUCKIN' LIFE PRETENDIN' TU BE UNCONSCIOUS...
... NOW FUCKIN' THINK!
I'M THINKIN', I'M THINKIN'.
SHE'S GERRIN' CLURSER, BAZ.
HOWAY... HOWAY... HOWAY... HOWAY...
I'M FINISHED.
FOT!
I'VE GORRIT, SID, MAN... THE FUCKIN' PORFECT WAY OOT!...

FUCKIN' LUCKY ESCAPE THAT, SID. THANKS TU MY QUICK THINKIN' EH?
NEXT TIME YU WANT A BLUR JOB, SID, GET YASEL' DOON PINK LANE WI' TWENTY POOND LIKE EVERY FUCKER ELSE.
SILENCE IN ZE RANKS!
The End.

THE HARDEST VIDEOS WE'VE EVER SOLD - BUT THAT'S NOT SAYING VERY MUCH

All these videos are absolutely un-cut as there is absolutely nothing in them remotely explicit enough to warrant censorship of any kind.

YOU WON'T HAVE SEEN ANYTHING LIKE IT IN ADULT VIDEOS BEFORE!

£27.95 ea. or 4 for £100

SEXTH FORM PREFECTS

What happens when two sexually frustrated blonde sixth form nymphettes find themselves alone in the dormitory on a hot summer's night with just a selection of sex toys to keep them company? We don't know, and you won't find out from this video starring a couple of bored looking 48 year-old slappers in wigs. Half-heartedly dressed as sixth form schoolgirls, they quickly get down to business on a bunk bed in the back of a warehouse in Peckham, disinterestedly rubbing each others' tits for eight minutes to a soundtrack of mains humming. And that's it. **Price £27.95.**

HOT, HARD 'N' HORNY

Big John is a plumber who is called out by a horny 36DD housewife to change the washer on her tap. When that job is done, she gives him another - a blow job! And she finds out he's got a 10 inch tool in his overalls. You really have to see it to believe it. However, you **don't** see it, just six minutes of the back of her head moving up and down intercut with close-ups of him screwing his face up. We guarantee you will be **shocked** by how much you have paid for this truly shit film. **Price £27.95.**

WARNING!
These videos are very unfulfilling, and we urge anyone who is easily disappointed not to buy them. They depict tame **SEXUAL ACTS,** in some cases of a blurred or wobbly nature that many viewers may find risible. It is not our intention to **AROUSE** or **EXCITE** the viewer, merely to mislead them into **PARTING** with their **HARD** earned cash without **BREAKING THE LAW** and indeed embarrass them into not asking for their **MONEY BACK.**

BUY NOW BEFORE WE'RE PROSECUTED UNDER THE TRADES DESCRIPTION ACT

WIDE OPEN AND WILLING

Cindy Smallpiece, a 38DD sex mad red-head just loves to dress up. She finds putting on her black fishnet stockings, split crotch panties and black stilettoes a real turn-on... but not as big a turn-on as taking them off! However, despite featuring heavily on the packaging, she's not actually in the video, which features a stripper with flu from Stoke Newington hurriedly taking her clothes off in the back of a warehouse in Clapham in return for fifty quid cash. With wow and flutter soundtrack of cheesy music from a battery operated cassette recorder, this will be one of the least erotic experiences of your life. **Price £27.95.**

EIGHT WAY SEX PLAY

When four well hung studs meet four big titted chicks, the permutations are incalculable. It's everyone's ultimate fantasy, as the guys and girls do it in every possible (and some impossible!) position including sandwich, 'A' and 'O'. This is the hardest film we've ever seen, but due to heavy re-editing for legal reasons, it's unlikely to be the hardest **you've** ever seen. Shot in the seventies on super 8 and recently transferred to video by projecting it onto a warehouse door, the whole sorry four minutes is accompanied by the sound of the projector turning over and somebody reversing a van outside. Just as something vaguely sexy starts to happen, the film sticks and melts before your very eyes. Deeply dreadful. **Price £27.95.**

With every order we receive, we'll send you, absolutely FREE a quality love doll. Always willing and always available, these sex dolls will fulfill your every need, providing you're turned on by orange paddling pool vinyl and that you're not too dizzy after twenty minutes blowing it up. Well stacked with tits that look and feel like the half footballs that they are and equipped with 3 (yes 3!) inviting orrifices, each with a razor sharp welded plastic seam guaranteed to cut your old man to ribbons in the unlikely event that you get aroused enough to try and shag it.
Buy ALL 4 videos, and receive the deluxe model with vaginal vibral unit plus vibrating throb control mouth, which will do nothing for you but will certainly affect next door's television reception, leaving them in no doubt as to what you're up to. Requires 24 AA batteries (not supplied).

Yes! I want you to have my home address and credit card details. Please send me the following videos.

- ☐ SEXTH FORM PREFECTS
- ☐ HOT HARD 'N' HORNY
- ☐ WIDE OPEN AND WILLING
- ☐ EIGHT WAY SEX PLAY

Send to: Randy Bollocks Porn Products, PO Box 1, Peckham.

Name................ ...Address......................... Credit Card No. ....

If I'm not completely satisfied, and I won't be I can return the videos for you to sell to some other poor sod with full nuts. I will recieve a cheque for the full amount drawn on the account of *Randy Bollocks Porn Products* with pictures of dildos drawn on it and the words ' Porn Video Refund' written on in big letters, which I will not dare take into my bank. I accept that this is my own fault.

Jobs for the boys...
Mechanics Reg Dawson and Trevor Todd were just opening up at the start of another busy week at Joskin Bros. Garage...
I don't know what's wrong with it. It's making a dreadful noise.
I bet your engine's shagged, Mrs. Collins. We're used to women shaggin' their engines, aren't we, Reg?
Aye. Don't worry, darlin'. We'll have a look at it. Come and pick it up at five o'clock.
Five o'clock? We'll never get it done by five. We're snowed under.
I know, but the new lad we took on, Dave, starts today, remember?
Oh, yeah!
Suddenly...
Wotcha, lads!
Oh, ayup, Dave. We were just talking about you.
I'm afraid we're going to chuck you in at the deep end, Dave. Can you fit a new gangle pin in this motor for us?
Oh, yeah. A Satsuma Castanet, Mk II. That'll take a reverse spline 3/4 hex gangle pin on the underside of the rear glib shaft. Got to offer it up blind.
By Christ, Reg! He knows his stuff.
Too right. I think it was a good move taking him on.

Shortly...
Finished, Reg. What do you want me to do now?
Oh, hang on a second, Dave. I'm having a bit of trouble getting this thing started. I don't understand it.
GVN 320D
Let's have a look, now...
...Ah! Here's the trouble. You've got cross polarity on your adjustable trumpets.
Eh!?!
There! Try it now.
VROOOOOM!
Amazing. It's running like a Swiss clock.
Later...
Eight sugars in your tea is it, Dave?
Erm, no thanks. None. I've got my own sweetener.
Ponies
Phwoar!!.. Look at the tits on that! Imagine a face full of them eh, Dave!
Gawd, Blimey!
Erm... yeah ... er... great!
FRUIT 'N' NUT
Listen, Dave. Fancy coming to the pub with me and Trev tonight?
Yeah! We're going to see some strippers, chat some birds up, drink loads of pints and then get big tattoos done on our chests.
Erm.. sorry, I can't. I'm er.. watching football.
STAR
That's funny. There's no football on tonight.
Hmm!
MINI

Later that day...
Aw, fuck! This is the wrong size. Throw us a size 10 spanner will you. Dave?
Erm... erm... It's okay. I'll bring it across.
No, just throw it.
Well, I'd really rather bring...
Look, Dave. Stop making a fuss and just chuck him the fuckin' spanner!
Well, here goes...!
Heurgh!
TONK!
CLING!
TINK!
Erm... cheers, Dave.
Did you see that?
Yeah! He threw that spanner like a bloody woman.
He did. And have you ever noticed how he always goes in the cubicle when he has a piss?
Yeah! And I've never seen him scratch his nuts or hockle on the floor.
Hmmm! Something's not right.

Anyhow, this needs some oil.
Yeah!
Here, Dave, do you know where the oil is?
Yeah! It's in my locker.
Great! I'll just go and get it.
NO! WAIT!
Eh!?! Soft toys? Perfume? Tampons? David Cassidy? Whose is all this stuff, Dave?
It's mine...
...and my name's not Dave...
...it's DAPHNE!
WHAT?!!....
...IT'S A LASS!!
But... but... why? What's going on?
I needed a job. I'm a good mechanic, but I knew you'd never take on a girl...
...so I disguised myself as a man.

I'm sorry. I'll clear my locker straight away.
No, wait! You're right, we wouldn't have taken on a girl. And our sexist attitudes would have lost us the best mechanic we've ever seen. You've certainly taught us a lesson. You've taught us that sexism has no place at work, at home or anywhere.
There's a job for you in this garage for as long as you want it, Daphne.
Thanks. I won't let you down.
Well, come on then. Mrs. Collins will be here to pick her car up any minute. Back it out into the street, Daphne and I'll make the bill up.
Okay, Trev.
Well, I've learnt something today, Reg.
Me too! I've learnt that women are equally as good as men, even in traditionally male dominated fields, and it's just prejudice and ignorance from people like us that stop them from competing on equal terms.
That's right, Reg.
VROOOOM!
N32 TTN
KER-SHUNT!
BANG! CRASH!
TINKLE! TINKLE!
GB
FAR 484K
N32 TTN
Boo! Hoo! Boo! Hoo! I'm sorry.. I'm so sorry.
Fuck me! Women drivers, eh!?
Aye!
The End

ONCE AGAIN, OUR CHAMPION OF CHAUVINISM IS PATROLLING THE SUBURBS OF BIGTOWN CITY - ON THE LOOKOUT FOR ANY MAN IN PERIL. ANY MAN WHO NEEDS...
CAPTAIN SEXIST
PHWOOAR! THIS SEX-RAY VISION IS FUCKIN' GREAT! LOOK AT THE JUBBLIES ON HER! GAW! YOU DON'T GET MANY OF THEM TO THE POUND!
BOLLOCKS! SHE'S GONE INTO THE BEDROOM. LET'S SEE WHAT'S HAPPENING NEXT DOOR!
...YOU SIT THERE ALL BLOODY DAY WHILST I SLAVE AWAY...
I'M TRYING TO WATCH THIS!
OH-OH! TROUBLE!
WELL NOW IT'S YOUR BLOODY TURN! I'M OFF TO THE BINGO. AND WHEN I COME BACK I WANT THIS PLACE TIDIED UP AND MY TEA READY!
AW BLOODY HELL FIRE.
SLAM!
FEAR NOT!
CAPTAIN SEXIST! IS IT REALLY YOU?
IT'S ME! CHAMPION OF THE DOWNTRODDEN MALE!
YOUR MISSUS IS A BIT OF AN OLD BOOT ISN'T SHE?
YES. AND IF I DON'T DO AS SHE SAYS SHE'LL HAVE MY KNACKERS ON HER HAT WHEN SHE GETS BACK!
...BUT I JUST WANT TO WATCH TELLY. WHAT AM I GOING TO DO?
JUST LEAVE IT TO THE SEXIST CAPTAIN WONDER!
ZOK!
I PUT HER BEST DRESS IN THE BOIL-WASH... WITH YOUR PURPLE PANTS!
GASP!
POW!
...HER GRANNY'S HEIRLOOM BONE CHINA DINNER SERVICE... IN THE DISHWASHER!
WOW!
WHAM!
WATCH! AS I CLEAN HER TEFLON FRYING PAN WITH A BRILLO PAD!
KRETCH!
FAR TOO MUCH SALT IN THE POTATOES!
WOW CAPTAIN! YOU REALLY ARE A MAN-MARVEL!
LATER...
...I LEAVE YOU IN CHARGE FOR FIVE BLOODY MINUTES AND WHAT DO YOU DO - YOU RUIN ME BEST DRESS! AND THAT CHINA TEA SERVICE - WHAT'S LEFT OF IT - BELONGED TO MY GRANNY, YOU USELESS BLOODY IDIOT!
I'M SORRY LOVE. I DIDN'T THINK...
YOU NEVER THINK - YOU USELESS GREAT LUMP!
...WELL IN FUTURE YOU DON'T DO ANYTHING! IN FACT - YOU DON'T SET FOOT IN MY KITCHEN AGAIN, DO YOU HEAR ME? YOU JUST SIT IN THAT CHAIR LIKE THE USELESS BLOODY SLOB YOU ARE!
THANK-YOU CAPTAIN SEXIST... WHEREVER YOU ARE.
THE END

Sid the Sexist in... THE LANDLORD OF OZ
BAR
OZ
DISCO PUB
HAPPY HOUR
12 SHOTS FOR A QUID
... ANYWAYS, DIVVEN'T FRET. I'LL JUST STICK A TOFFEE ON THE END OF IT, AN' WHEN YEE START CHEWIN, I'LL STOP PUSHIN!
TUT!
REET, I'M GANNIN' FORRA PISS. LISTEN, PET, KEEP IT WARM AN' WET FORRUZ COZ I'M COMMIN' BACK FORRA SNIFF. YOU'VE FUCKIN' SCORED.
GENTS
GENTS
?

WHERE THE FUCK AM I? LOOK AT AAL THE TREES AN' FLOOAZ. I'VE NEVER SEEN OWT LIKE IT IN ME LIFE. I MUST BE IN GATESHEED.
THAT'S REET, SIDOTHY. YOU'RE IN GATESHEED.
BUT I NEED TO GET BACK TO OZ'S. I NEVER HAD ME PISS. AN' THERE'S A LASS GOT US ON A PROMISE... ... WHICH WAY DO I GAN?
THAT WAY, SIDOTHY. FOLLOW THE YELLOW SICK ROAD.
SMASHIN. I'M FUCKIN' BUSTIN! -COME ON, TYSON!
I'M OFF TO SEE THE LANDLORD, THE WONDERFUL LANDLORD OF OZ, I REALLY, REALLY NEED A PISS, AND HIS ARE THE NEAREST BOGS. THEY REALLY ARE THE NEAREST BOGS, TO STRAIN YOUR GREENS AND DROP YOUR LOGS, YOUR LOGS, YOUR LOGS, YOUR LOGS, YOUR LOGS, YOUR LO-O-O-O-O-O-O-O-O-GS...
WOW! IT'S A TIN BAZ!
HOW, TIN BAZ. WHAT Y'DEEIN?
SIDOTHY, MAN. I'VE PULLED A TOP TIN BORD. RIVETED TITS, BRILLO PAD PUBES, THE LOT!... ... ONLY THING IS, ME FUCKIN' POOND'S GOT JAMMED IN THIS BASTAD BLOB MACHINE!
DANISH BLUE (CHEESE FLAVOUR)
ORIGINAL (RUBBER FLAVOUR)
Y'KNAA!... IT MAKES US FEEL LIKE SINGIN!
OH, I'D SHAG THIS METAL WOMAN, TILL ME NUTS THEY WERE A CUMMIN' WITH ME SHINY METAL KNOB, I WOULD GIVE HER SUCH A BANGIN' I WOULD SET HER TITS A CLANGIN' IF I ONLY HAD A BLOB!
TOOT! TOOT!
DIVEN'T FRET YOURSELF, TIN BAZ, COME WI'ME. I'M GANNIN' TO THE PUB FORRA PISS. THEY'VE GOT A BLOB MACHINE ON THE WALL O'THE BOGS.

FOLLOW THE YELLOW SICK ROAD, FOLLOW THE YELLOW SICK ROAD, FOLLOW, FOLLOW, FOLLOW, FOLLOW, FOLLOW THE YELLOW SICK ROAD. ♫
OH, LOOK, TIN BAZ, IT'S A SCAREJOE.
OH, YES, SIDOTHY.
HOW JOE, WHAT'S WRANG?
I'M FUCKIN' CHURKIN' FOR A DRINK, SIDOTHY MAN. THE OFFY'S SHUT AND I WANT TO GET PISSED.
I WOULD LOVE TO GET A ROUND IN, ♪ GIVE MY LIVER A GOOD POUNDIN' OH, MY BALANCE I WOULD LOSE. I WOULD START SEEING DOUBLE, AN' I'D CAUSE ALOT OF TROUBLE IF I HAD A LOT OF BOOZE.
WELL, COME WITH US, SCAREJOE, WE'RE OFF TO SEE THE LANDLORD OF OZ.
HE SELLS SMASHIN' LAGER.
SOMEWHERE OVER THE TYNE BRIDGE, THERE'S A PLACE, WHERE YOU CAN PISS, AND BUY BLOBS AN' DRINK, ♪ 'TILL YOU'RE OFF YOUR FACE... ♪
ROOOOOOAR!
HACK! COUGH! SPLUTTER! HAS ANYBODY GOT ANY TABS?
SORRY, BOBCAT. THEZ NAIRN OF US GOT NEY TABS.
FUCKIN' TYPICAL! CHURKIN' FORRA SMURK, AN' NEY FUCKAZ GOT ANY TABS.

I WOULD LOVE A NICE BIG REGAL, 'COS I SMOKE EM LIKE A BEAGLE, OH, THAT REALLY WOULD BE FAB, I WOULD COUGH UP MY LEFT LUNG, AND GET CANCER OF THE TONGUE, ♫ IF I ONLY HAD A TAB. ♪
DIVVEN'T WORRY, BOBCAT. THE LANDLORD OF OZ'S HAS GOT A MACHINE IN THE CORRIDOR. COME WITH US.
WE'RE OFF TO SEE THE LANDLORD, THE FUCKING GREAT LANDLORD OF OZ, ♫
♪ AND I'LL GET THE CHANCE TO HAVE ME WEE IN HIS GENTLEMEN'S OOTSIDE BOGS, ♫
♪ AND I'LL GET TO BUY A PACKET OF THREE,
AND TWENTY REGAL JUST FOR ME, ♫
AND I'LL GET PISSED BECAUSE, BECAUSE, BECAAAAAAAUSE... BECAUSE OF THE VERY STRONG BEER HE DOES!
DE DIDDLY DIDDLY DUM.
LOOK! THERE IT IS! OZ! I'LL GET ME PISS!
I'LL GET ME BLOBS!
I'LL GET ME TABS!
AN' I'LL GET OFF ME FUCKIN' FACE!
BAR
SHIT! IT'S LOCKED UP. WHERE'S THE BASTAD LANDLORD?
THERE HE IS, IN THAT BALLOON!

McO'DOUGLE'S TRAVELLING FAIR
YES, I'M FUCKIN' OFF HOME IN THIS BALLOON, JUST LIKE IN THE WIZARD OF OZ.
BASTAD!! WE'VE COME ALL THIS WAY ALANG THE YELLOW SICK ROAD...
♪ DING DONG! THE PUB IS SHUT! THE PUB IS SHUT! THE PUB IS SHUT! ♪
FUCK OFF, SCAREJOE, THIS IS SERIOUS, Y'THICK CUNT.
LISTEN, I'LL CLIMB UP THESE BARRELS INTO THAT WINDEE, AN I'LL LET YUZ AAL IN. WE'LL HAVE THE PUB TO WU'SELLS. WE'LL HAVE THE WORLD'S PREMIER ALL-NEET LOCK-IN.
WOW! OZ REALLY IS A TRULY MAGICAL PLACE.
GAN ON, SIDOTHY. GIVE IT SOME.
WOBBLE!
WOBBLE!
CHEAP LAGER
WHAAAA!
SMECK!
SIDOTHY, SIDOTHY, ARE YEE AALREET?
WAA! FUCK! ME HEED!

SID, SID, ARE YEE AALREET, MAN?
TIN BAZ... SCAREJOE... BOBCAT... AND TYSON TOO... TYSON TOO... TYSON TOO
WHAT THE FUCK ARE YEE ON ABOOT, SID?
WHAT HAPPENED? WHERE AM I?
THIS BIG CUNT TWATTED YOU.
AYE. FUCKIN' LAMPED YOU ONE, SID.
AYE... AN' I'LL LAMP YI' SOME MORE IF Y'TRY CHATTIN WOR LASS UP AGAIN.
BAR
YEE! OOT!
DOOOAGHH! I'VE PISSED MESELF.
THE END

600 years of aesthetic femininity

FOR CENTURIES, the World's great artists have drawn their inspiration from women's tits. From Leonardo to Picasso, from Rembrandt to Rolf Harris, knockers have been one of the enduring themes to which the creative genius has returned time and again.

Now, the Royal Male invites you to join in celebrating 600 years of churns in art. Our new portfolio of postage stamps features some of the most beautiful and timeless headlamps selected from the greatest paintings in the World's most magnificent collections. They're yours to cherish in the privacy of your own lavatory for years to come.

7p; Agnolo Bronzino - *Man squeezing woman's left tit, 1545.* (Artichoke Gallery).
8p; Auguste Renoir - *Les grande baps de baigneuses, 1887.* (Craft Cheese Gallery).
9p; Paul Gauguin - *Nudie bird having a kip, 1897.* (Shipton Bequest).
10p; Sandro Botticelli - *The Charlies of Venus, 1485.* (Magic Roundabout Gallery).
11p; Pablo Picasso - *Three wonky topless birds, 1925.* (The Tate & Lyle Gallery).
12p; Michelangelo - *Dolly bird with knocker out, 1500.* (The Vision On Gallery).
£8.23; Paul Cezanne - *Baywatch, 1900.* (Collection of Chubby Brown).
£9.06; Reg Ingres - *Stripper from Nottingham, 1806.* (Louvre Door Gallery).

Available November 1st from your Post Office, Newsagent or Mucky Bookshop

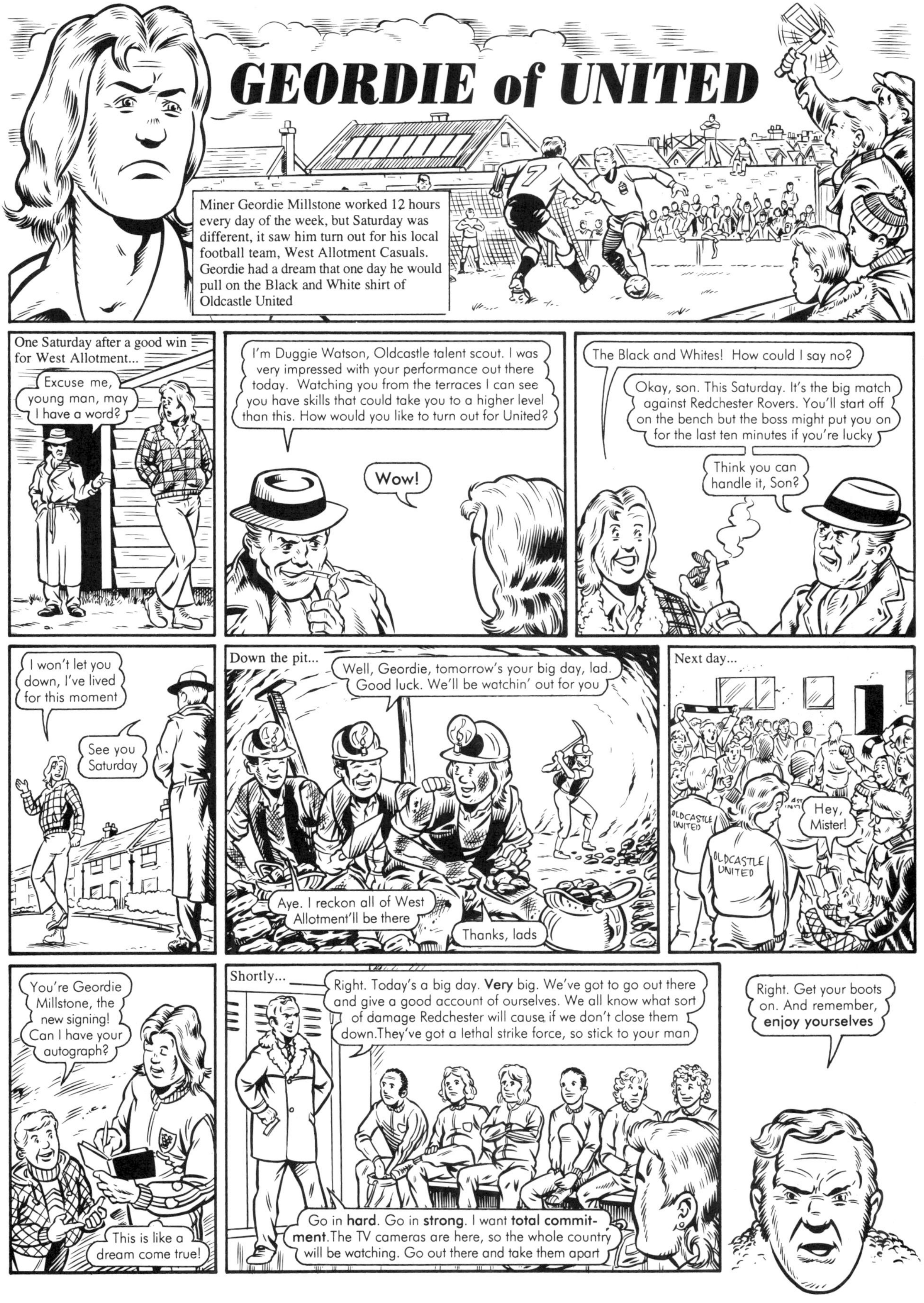
GEORDIE of UNITED
Miner Geordie Millstone worked 12 hours every day of the week, but Saturday was different, it saw him turn out for his local football team, West Allotment Casuals. Geordie had a dream that one day he would pull on the Black and White shirt of Oldcastle United
One Saturday after a good win for West Allotment...
Excuse me, young man, may I have a word?
I'm Duggie Watson, Oldcastle talent scout. I was very impressed with your performance out there today. Watching you from the terraces I can see you have skills that could take you to a higher level than this. How would you like to turn out for United?
Wow!
The Black and Whites! How could I say no?
Okay, son. This Saturday. It's the big match against Redchester Rovers. You'll start off on the bench but the boss might put you on for the last ten minutes if you're lucky
Think you can handle it, Son?
I won't let you down, I've lived for this moment
See you Saturday
Down the pit...
Well, Geordie, tomorrow's your big day, lad. Good luck. We'll be watchin' out for you
Aye. I reckon all of West Allotment'll be there
Thanks, lads
Next day...
OLDCASTLE UNITED
Hey, Mister!
OLDCASTLE UNITED
You're Geordie Millstone, the new signing! Can I have your autograph?
This is like a dream come true!
Shortly...
Right. Today's a big day. **Very** big. We've got to go out there and give a good account of ourselves. We all know what sort of damage Redchester will cause if we don't close them down. They've got a lethal strike force, so stick to your man
Go in **hard**. Go in **strong**. I want **total commitment**. The TV cameras are here, so the whole country will be watching. Go out there and take them apart
Right. Get your boots on. And remember, **enjoy yourselves**

ROAR!!
Pheep!
How! Yuz are aall a bunch o'fuckin' red wankers!
The Oldcastle boys get the unruly behaviour underway. Some nice solid abuse to start off with. Gone straight for route one there...
What's your fuckin' problem then, y'Geordie bastard!?
..but the Reds have replied with a pretty respectable counter-attack...
Fuck off! D'yu wanna make summat of it?
Ye can stick ya black puddin's up yer arses y' fuckin' Lancashire twats!
How! Ref! Y'fat cunt!
...Oh! He's switched the play and found the referee with an inch-perfect forty-yard pie...
...and he's got away with that one, the copper was unsighted there...
...and Oldcastle are really fuelled up. They've been drinking all afternoon...
...veteran skipper Ronnie Thompson passed a late drunkenness test. He's been out for two weeks after taking a nasty curry at Blackborough last month during a pre-season unfriendly....
...and Redchester's star striker Vinegar Jones is going for a shot from all of 25 yards!...
LAGER
...Oh! And he's hit the woodwork!...
STOTT!
...but he's followed it in with a tremendous header! Pace and accuracy...
KNUT!
...and the Oldcastle skipper's down. It looks like it'll be a free-kick to Redchester. The ball's well placed for a right-footed inswinger...
...Jones takes it quickly. Oh my word, he's hit that ball like an express train!

And the Oldcastle trainer is on with the magic sponge... the copper's insisting he's carried off. Oh dear, this looks bad for Thomson...
...Oldcastle only have untried new boy Geordie Millstone on the bench, but they've got no choice. Thomson's afternoon is over. They're warming the lad up
OLDCASTLE UN
Go on son! Finish it! Get it down your neck! Drink lager! Drink lager! Go out there! Them Redchester boys...one of them call your mam a whore!...
I'll kick their fuckin' heads in!
That's it Son! Keep that spirit up
You're goin' home in a fu-kin' am-bu-lance!
...Oh, and the new boy's straight into the action, showing good use of both feet. He's turned his man brilliantly. Tremendous skill!
What a debut! This boy is unstoppable! He's taken out five Redchester lads on a 25-terrace solo run with a plywood hoarding! What tenacity...
The police have closed him down, but his talents are amazing. He's managed a 3-coppers' hat-trick on his inauguration...
...and a textbook arrest to cap it off! What a way to open your criminal record! These scenes will surely be remembered as some of the most disgraceful ever seen at this ground!
OLDCASTL
The next day...
Look, Mum. I've put Oldcastle back on the map! We're out of Europe...thanks to me!
I'm so proud of you, Son
OLDCASTLE NEWS
THE UNACCEPTABLE FACE OF FOOTBALL
UNITED BARRE FROM ALL INTER COMPETITIONS
Epilogue - After an unequalled career of over 800 appearances in court for Oldcastle, and 50 arrests for England, the people of Oldcastle pulled down a statue in Geordie Millstone's honour

Your Medical Questions Answered

Dear Dr. Smutt,
How much fags is it safe to smoke?
Frank.
Walford

Dr. Smutt replies
It is safe to smoke upwards of 80 or 100 tabs a day. My grandad smoked 270 a day from the age of six, and he was killed running for a bus when he was 104. His brother, who did'nt never smoke was ran over by a bus when he was 28.

Dr. Smutt is a proper doctor and knows what he's on about

For everyone life is difficult sometimes. But for people like Stanley it's difficult *all* the time.

For people like Stanley (not his real name) a trip to the shop (it's Sidney) to buy some tabs can turn into a nightmare. An evening at the pub often ends in an ambulance trip to hospital. Taking a girl to the cinema will almost certainly end in him being kicked in the pods. Society shuns him, people avoid him in the street.
Because, through no fault of his own, Stanley is a twat.
Shortly after his birth, he began showing the first signs of the dismal personality which now leaves him a sad and pathetic laughing-stock amongst his peers and, more importantly to Stanley, deeply repellent to women.
Because of his boorish, unpleasant behaviour, no self-respecting woman would touch him with a bargepole. There is nothing that can be done to change his personality and give him a chance of scoring. The future is bleak. As he gets older, he'll simply become more of a twat. Deep down he knows he'll never break his duck.

But you can help make Stanley's life more bearable:

£1 will buy him a week's viewing of the Fantasy Channel on Satellite
£5 will buy a glossy top shelf scud mag and a box of man-size tissues
£10 will buy a copy of Sluts International on VHS
£15 will pay for a three minute phone call to a sex line terminating in Ulan Bator
£50 will get him a deeply regrettable blow job off a woman in a pub car park

Think about people like Stanley when you're on the job. And please help

Fuck off. I'm not giving any money to twats like that. ☐ I enclose nowt.
Signed.......................Name ....
Address...
Send to: Sexist Appeal. FREEPOST. Leeds

Less than 98% of the money we raise is eaten up by administration and the staff Christmas party.

Tired of being slapped in the face by women for your suggestive comments? *Then rise above them!*

Now it's easy to shout at and embarrass women in complete safety without the danger of redress with the JEER-STAGE. Easily erected, the four storey scaffold, available for the first time to the amateur allows **professional quality** verbal assault to be achieved from even the novice DIY builder or handyman.

Each JEER-STAGE comes complete with a hard hat and phrase book of the most coarse insults and wolf calls used on today's building sites.

Please rush me one of those four-storey JEER-STAGE things.
I enclose £.................
Name..........Address......................

JEER-STAGE Ltd, PO Box 1. Hull.

You'll never feel clean again
after a stay at the
TIPTON
SHAGNASTY HOTEL

THE SHAGNASTY HOTEL, nestling in the heart of the West Midlands provides the perfect hideaway for a sordid hour frantically poking that special someone you've just picked up. At the Tipton Shagnasty, we boast:

*** PAPER THIN WALLS * MAPS OF AFRICA ON ALL BED LINEN**
*** THIEVING STAFF * SMELL OF PISS THROUGHOUT**
*** HAPPY HOUR OVERCHARGING AT THE BAR**
*** RAT SHIT * NO ROOM SERVICE**

40 imaginatively appointed bedroom suites, crammed into a standard two bedroomed end terraced house. A single room costs from as little as 50p a minute for two people. There's no reservations necessary so come stay with us and get away from it all for 15 minutes or so.

spake unto him out of the window in a voice of thun-
der saying, Begone 8 Ace who is begat of 32 Eiger.
34 And he took up his tins and dwelt in his shed.

CHAPTER 14.

AND it came to pass that on the seventh day there
came from the North East Sidney, who was begat
of his mam who dwelt in the land of Byker.
2 And he came down unto the town of New Castle
to go to the pub to seek his friends.
3 And he came upon Joe who is begat of Big Joe
and Bob and Barry, who is called Baz. And they
looked upon their glasses and saw that they were bar-
ren. And Sidney was cast forth unto the bar that they
be replenished even unto the fourth pint. For it was
written that it was His shout.
4 And Sidney did buy the round and some crisps of
salt and vinegar and cheeses and onions and the
scratchings of the swine of the fields, even unto two
bags. And the others who were gathered looked upon
the round and they saw that it was good.
5 So they sat back and did drink deeply of the lagers
and were becalmed. And they began to cast their lech-
erous eyes upon the women of the pub and they were
tempted for they had fashioned their garments one
cubit above the knee and did leave little to the imagi-
nation, I can tell you.
6 And their heads were full of unclean thoughts.
And Sidney beheld a woman's jugs and did covet
them for they were indeed smashing. And he nudged
Barry who is called Baz and passed adulterous com-
ment and blasphemed saying he wouldn't mind a face-
ful of them.
7 But Baz did mock him, saying that he was virgin
and chaste and celibate, and that he hath known not a
woman though be he one score and eight.
8 Yet did Sidney answer and spake unto those who
sat with him, saying these words were untrue, and that
the women he hath known were multitude and num-
bered more than the lilies of the field or the birds of
the air.
9 But his friends laughed and reproached him say-
ing, cease with these falsehoods, Sidney, for we are
wise to your ways. And they accused him saying that
he did take up the Freeman's catalogue and seek the
bra pages and spill his seed upon the ground. And
they pointed at him and sang cherry boy, cherry boy
10 And Sidney rose up and great was his anger.
11 And he rebuked them in an terrible voice, say-
ing that they were all a bunch of cunts. But yet did
they mock him and great was his woe for he knew in
his heart that it was true
12 And in his wrath he did spill the pint of Dave,
who is called Mental who sat at the table on his right
hand and his pint was cast upon the sticky carpet. And
Mental who had a head of skin looked upon it and
great was his displeasure. And Sidney spake to him a
parable; Behold, for I want not any trouble. But
Mental had got the mist, and lo, the mist was red.
And he smiled not upon Sidney, but smote him an
mighty blow in the teeth.
13 And again.
14 And thrice did he lamp Sidney whose fall was as
that of a sack of spuds and great was his suffering.
15 And they heared the voice of the LANDLORD
standing behind the bar. And he was sore vexed and
spake unto them in a loud voice saying, Yeez lot, oot.
16 And Sidney and Joe who is begat of Big Joe and
Bob and Barry who is called Baz were cast out into the
car park. And there was much cursing of the name of
Sidney and much gnashing of teeth and they wished
pestilence upon his head.

CHAPTER 15.

AND it came to pass that after holding counsel they
did reach a covenant that they maketh their
passage to the house of Ke-Bab, by the bus station.
And so they did.
2 And they entered the house. And they looked
upon the kebab revolving on the altar and did ask of
themselves what was in it.
3 And Baz spoke saying that it was made of the
nads and the lips and eyelids of the goat and the cow
and the sheep and the cat and all the unclean parts
thereof, even unto the chopper and ringpiece.
4 And great was the plague of flies upon the kebab.
And the price of the kebabs was one pound and nine
and ninety.
5 And Sidney and Joe who is begat of Big Joe and
Bob and Barry who is called Baz spoke saying, Four
kebabs pal. And the shopkeeper was called Stavros.
6 And Stavros said, Seven pound and six and nine-
ty, matey peeps. And he began preparations for their
feast and he did scratch his nuts and take the unleav-
ened bread.
7 And Sidney spoke another parable unto his three
disciples; Verily I say unto you, That Dave who is
called Mental was geet lucky, for had the LAND-
LORD not stepped in, yea would I surely have slain
the baldy fucker.
8 And they heared a voice and the voice said, Oh
yeah? And they turned about them and beheld Dave
who is called Mental, for he had likewise journeyed to
the house of Ke-Bab.
9 And Sidney's raiments of Levi became besoiled.
10 And he spoke another parable saying; Hello
Dave who is called Mental. I was just talking about
another Dave who is called Mental.
11 But Dave who is called Mental believed not
Sidney's falsehood and great was his wrath.
12 And mighty was the smoting that Sidney took
up the bracket and elsewise. And Joe who is begat of
Big Joe and Bob and Barry who is called Baz stepped
not in for Sidney, but did look at their footwear. They
denied Sidney and He was forsaken.

CHAPTER 16.

AND it came to pass that Sidney was put upon a
litter. And Joe who is begat of Big Joe and Bob
and Barry who is called Baz did journey with him to
the land of the Royal General Infirmary, whereupon

SID the SEXIST
DOON the SMURK
THE FOX AND HOOND
MORE FOUL-MOUTHED FUNNIES WITH YOUR FOUR-LETTER FRIENDS
... SHARON STALLURNE, SHE'S BEIN' QUESTIONED BY THE COPPAZ, AN' SHE KEEPS CROSSIN' HER LEGS, AN SHE'S GOT NEE KNICKAZ ON, Y'CAN SEE HER MUFF, THE LOT!... FUCK ME! WHAT AN ACTRESS!
HOW, LOOK! BAZ, IT'S YOUR DAVE.
OH, AYE! HE MUST'VE JUST GOT BACK FROM LONDON. HE'S BEEN DOON ON THE SITES FOR TWO MONTHS.
HOW, DAVEY BOY! BACK AWA THE TOON, EH?
AYE, SID. THERE'S NOWT LIKE COMIN' AWA THE BRIDGE.
AYE!
MIND, IT'S YOUR ROOND, THOUGH, BUT...
... TWO MONTH ON THE SITES... Y'MUST BE FUCKIN' HEAVIN' WI' SPONDS.
FUCK THAT! I HAVEN'T GOT TWO HA'PENNIES T'RUB TOGETHER.
EH? BUT I THOUGHT THEM JOBS WAS CASH IN HAND.
OH, AYE. CASH IN HAND AALREET...
... IT WUZ IN ME HAND, THEN ME BAALLS SEEN THAT IT WENT STRITE OOT THE END O' ME OLD MAN.
WHADDAYA MEAN, LIKE?
WELL, THERE'S ME AN' SIX OTHER GEORDIES AALL SHACKED UP IN THIS FUCKIN' CARAVAN ON THE SITE. WE TRIED GANNIN' TU THE PUBS, BUT THE FUCKIN' BEER'S AAFUL, AN' IT TOOK ABOOT TWO 'OOAZ T'GET A ROOND IN.
Y'SEE, THEY CANNAT UNDASTAND A WORD YE SAY. IT WUZ FUCKIN' DIRE. WE JUST SAT AROOND THE CARAVAN, NEE TELLY OR NOWT. MIND, ONE O' THE LADS HAD KER-PLUNK.
I TELL YUZ, I WAS IN FUCKIN' TEARS AFTER A WEEK. I WENT TU THE PHURN BOX TU CAALL ME MAM, ONLY WHEN I GOT THERE...
... THERE WAS AALL THESE CARDS AALL AWA THE WAALL.
FUCK ME!!
TOO FUCKIN' RIGHT, SID! THAT'S WHAT I THOUGHT. SUR I RANG A ONE UP.
ROXANNE
SHE WAS FUCKIN' NECTAR! SUR I GANS WITH ANOTHER ONE THE NEXT NEET. NEXT THING I KNAA, I CANNAT FUCKIN' STOP MESEL'. EVERY FUCKIN' NEET I WUZ HUMPIN'...
... TWICE OF A SATURDUR.
LAYIN' BRICKS OF A DAYTIME, LAYIN' LASSES ON A NIGHT TIME. IT'S A MIRACLE I NEVER PEGGED IT.
FUCKIN' HELL.
ME FUCKIN' BUILDING POOND WAS GERRIN' DEMOLISHED AS FAST AS I MADE THE CUNT.

ON ME LAST NEET, I HAD A HUNDRED POOND LEFT, JUST ENOUGH FOR A PROZZER AN'A TRAIN YEM...
...SUR I HAD TWO PROZZIES AN' HITCH-HIKED.
FUCKIN' HELL... WHARRA YU DRINKIN', DAVEY?
THANKS SID, BUT I'VE GORRA GAN DOON WARD 34. GOT A BIT OF A DURSE, LIKE...
SKRIT! SKRIT! SKRIT! SKRIT!
... MUST'VE GORRIT OFF A BOG SEAT, DORTY BASTARDS DOON LONDON, MAN.
TA-RA THEN, LADS.
EEEH, FUCKIN' HELL, LOOK AT THIS 'UN... EIGHTEEN YEAR OLD VORGIN IT SEZ HERE. PULL THE OTHER ONE.
AYE. IT'D BE MORE LIKE PUSHIN' A WOODBINE UP THE TYNE TUNNEL.
FUCK ME!
THIS ONE'S A SWEDISH PORN STAR.
IF SHE'S A FUCKIN' PORN STAR, THEN I'M A DUTCHMAN...
... AND BEFORE Y'ASK JOE, I'M NOT A DUTCHMAN.
IT'S FUCKIN SAD, REALLY. JUST GIVIN' SOME LASS YER WEDGE SO AS SHE LETS YU ON.
AYE. THEN PURKIN' A DIFFERENT ONE THE NEXT NEET. SAD.
FUCKIN' AAFUL...
...I'VE NEVER PAID FORRA FUCK IN ME LIFE, AN' I NEVER WILL.
I DIVVEN'T NEED TO... I PULL ENOUGH BLART WITHOOT GETTIN' ME WALLET OOT, THANKYOU VERY MUCH.
AYE. YUD NEVER CATCH ME PAYIN' FOR TU GET ME END AWAY... NEVER.
AYE.
NEXT MORNING...
SED CLOSED
TICKETS FOR TODAYS TRAVEL
CLOSE
DAY RETURN TU LONDON, PLEASE.
IS THAT TABBIN' IT, BONNY LAD?
AYE. ON THE TABS.
FIFTY-SEVEN POOND. PLATFORM FOUR.
4
WAKE ME UP AT CATTERICK

!
ER...AALREET SID? ERM... OFF T' LONDON THEN, EH?
ERM... AYE. ... I'M GANNIN' TU SEE ME NANA.
OH..AYE... ME AN' AALL.
WHAT ABOOT YEE, ROBAT?
ERM, I'M GANNIN' T' THAT FUCKIN'...ERM... ART GALLERY...ERM...T'SEE SOME BRICKS. THEY'VE GOT A WHOLE FUCKIN' PILE OF 'EM. I'VE AALWEZ FANCIED SEEIN'... ERM... SOME BRICKS...LIKE.
AN' YEE JURSEPH?
ERM... SCIENCE... MUSEUM.
SOONDS FUCKIN' CANNY.
A-HEM!
COUGH!
THREE HOURS LATER...
REET THEN. I'M OFF TU ME NANA'S.
ERM...ME AN' AALL.
IT'S NOT OUR FAULT
AYE. ERM...ART GALLERY HERE I COME.
AYE ... AN' I'M OFF TO ERM... TO... TO... I'M OFF TO...
TO THE SCIENCE MUSEUM, JOE.
AYE. THAT'S IT.
SO...
TAXI
WANK1
WHERE TO, CHIEF?
ERM... SURHUR.
NOT FWOM WOWND 'ERE, ARE YA, CHIEF!?!
NAAH. I'M FROM THE TOON, NEWCASSEL, LIKE.
LISTEN, SOHO'S FACKIN' MILES FWOM 'ERE, GEORDIE, BAT I KNOW A SHAWT CAT.
KINGS CROSS
SCREECH!

'ERE, WOT'S 'APPENED T'YAW BLOKE THEN EH? FIFTEEN MILLION HE COST YA, AN' WOT'S 'E DAN? EH? FACK AWL, THAT'S WOT. TWO LEFT FEET 'E'S GOT, FACKIN' WABBISH. MIND YOU, 'E 'AD T'GET RID O' THAT COLE GEEZAH. I MEAN, I'M NO RACIST, BAT HE...
BLAAAR!!
FACK OFF AAHT OF IT!
TINK!
SCREEECH!
AN HOUR LATER...
...AN' THE FING IS, SHE'S STILL GOT AWL 'ER OWN TEEF. AN' SHE WAS 'ERE AWL FREW THE DARK DAYS OF THE BLITZ, SHE WAS, DODGIN' BLADDY DOODLEBAGS, NOT LIKE THAT FIWFY NORVERN TRAITER GRACIE WOTS'ER-BLADDY-NAME, GOIN' SWANNIN' OFF T'CAPRI TILL IT WAS ALL OVER...
PARP!
GERTCHA!
CROYDON 3 Miles
ANOTHER HOUR LATER...
...AN' I SEZ I SHOULD FACKIN' COCOA. BAT IT'S THESE FACKIN' MURDERERS THAT GET ME, I MEAN THEY DO A MURDER AN' GET PUT IN THE NICK AN' IT'S LIKE THE FACKIN' RITZ. I MEAN, I'D 'ANG 'EM I WOULD, I'D DO IT. I'D PULL THE FACKIN' LEVER MESEWF... FINK TWICE ABAAHT DOIN' ANAVVER MURDER THEN, THEY WOULD.
NEARLY THERE, CHIEF.
WELCOME TO BRIGHTON
ANOTHER HOUR LATER...
... GOT RID O' NATIONAL SERVICE THEY SHOULDN'T. I RECKON EVERYONE 'OO'S 18 SHOULD DO TWO YEARS NATIONAL SERVICE F'QUEEN AN' CANTRY. AP AT SIX, SQUARE BASHIN', SHININ' YER BOOTS WIV A SPOON. THAT'D SAWT 'EM AAHT. NEVER DID ME ANY 'ARM. MIND YOU, I DIDN'T DO IT, ON ACCAHNT OF ME FEET BEIN' FLAT, Y'SEE...
TAXI
ZZZZZ
AND ANOTHER...
...BAT THE REAL TRABBLE WIV THE YOOF OF TODAY IS, THAT THEY AIN'T GOT NO RESPECT FOR THE OWLD FOLKS, THEIR ELDERS AN' BETTERS, 'CAUSE THEY JAST DON'T...
BLAAAAR!
TAXI
WANK 1
GET YER FACKIN' EYES TESTED, GRANDAD!!
GAW! WOT ARE THEY LIKE, EH, SAM OF 'EM? MIND YOU, YOU'LL NEVER GUESS 'OO I 'AD IN THE BACK O' THIS TAXI LARST WEEK. NAAAH. GAW ON, 'AVE A GUESS...
... OOOH! 'ERE WE ARE, MATE. SOHO.
RIGHT THEN, LET'S 'AVE A BUTCHER'S... THAT'S TWO 'ANDRED AN' NINETY QUID PLEASE, JOHN. SORRY ABAAHT. TRAFFIC'S BLADDY MURDER, INNIT?
TAXI
WANK 1
HEH! HEH! HEH! FANKS A FACKIN' BANCH. YER BLEEDIN' NORVERN PONCE!
XXX CIN
GIRLS GIRLS GIRLS
PEEP SHOW £5
VR
OOOM!

SEX
NAKED GIRLS IN BED 50P
CINEMA-A-GO-GO XXX
FILTH! FILTH! FILTH!
ERM... ERM...
GIRLS ON SHOW
AALREET. AALREET. WUZ'VE AALL COME DOON FOR TU GET WUR URTS OFF PROZZERS.
ERM... WELL, ...AYE.
WELL... I'M HERE TO... ERM... TO... AYE. YER REET. BAZ.
I'M GANNIN' TU THE SCIENCE MUSEUM.
NAAH... Y'CAN STOP AALL YER SCIENCE MUSEUM SHITE, NOO, JOE MAN.
CAN I?... CHAMPION.
REET. SUR WUZ'RE AALL HERE TO PAY FOR WUR BIT SEXUAL ELATIONS...
... SUR CAN ANYONE LEND US SOME CASH, 'COZ THAT COCKNEY CUNT IN THE TAXI TOOK AALL MINE!
FUCK ME! IT'S EXPENSIVE DOON HERE. THE TAXI COST US AALL MY WEDGE AN' AALL.
WELCOME TU THE FUCKIN' CLUB.
SUR... HURLD ON.... WUZ'VE GOT NEE MONEY BETWEEN US? NOT A FUCKIN' BRASS FARTHIN'?
NAAH. HAD ON. I'VE GOT TEN POOND. WHY DIVVEN'T WUZ AALL HAVE A PINT, WAALK BACK TU THE STATION AN' GAN YEM?
FUCKIN' GOOD IDEA.
SUDDENLY...
FANCY A SHOW, LADS? TWO GIRLS, A GEEZA AN' A DONKEY. LIVE! ON STAGE. ONE O' THE GIRLS'S GOT A SNAKE.
DISGRACEFUL MUCK HERE NOW!
SEX
NAH THANKS MATE, WUV GORRA GET...
IT'S FREE LADS, SHOW'S STARTIN'. AN' I'VE GOT T' FILL THE THEATRE. THERE'S FOUR FRONT ROW SEATS LEFT, AN' IF I DON'T FILL 'EM I'LL GET THE BLADDY TIN-TACK. CAM IN LADS ... PLEASE!
FREE, EH?, WUR LUCK'S CHANGED! HAWAY IN LADS!
DID I SAY THE SHOWS STARTIN'? I MEAN IT STARTS IN HALF AN' HOUR. WHY DON'T YOU ALL HAVE A DRINK WHILE YOU WAIT?
AYE. I'VE GOT A THRURT AS DRY AS AN ARAB'S SANDAL, MAN.
SHORTLY...
FUCKIN' HELL...
WHEN'S THIS SHUR GANNA START?!
SORRY LADS. I'M AFRAID THE SHOW'S BEEN CANCELLED. THE DONKEY'S DEAD.
SO 'ERE'S YER DRINKS BILL, IF YOU WOULDNT MIND SETTLIN' AP.

WHAT THE FUCK!?
THE RUB-A-DUB CLUB
4 pints butter
€ 1400
FAWATEEN POOND FOR FAWA PINTS O' FIZZY PISS? FUCK OFF! I'M NOT PAYIN' FAWATEEN FUCKIN' POOND!
GET YERSELF BACK T'SCHOOL, GEORDIE...
...YER PAYIN' FOURTEEN HANDRED. AN' BEFORE YOU SAY ANYFINK, OUR PRICES ARE DISPLAYED BEHIND THE BAR — AS REQUIRED BY LAW — SO YOU SHOULDN'T 'AVE ORDERED IF YOU WASN'T PREPARED TO PAY OUR PRICES.
WHERE?...
WHERE'S THE PRICES?
BEHIND THE BAR!!...
...JUST ABOVE THE SKIRTIN' BOARD ON THE BACK OF A POSTAGE STAMP.
YOU'VE BEEN TOLD, NOW FACKIN' PAY AP!
HOWAY MAN, WUZ'RE FUCKIN' BARRASIC...
...BUT LISTEN... WUZ'LL AALL GAN T'THE BANK, GET AALL YER CASH, AN' COME STRITE BACK, MAN... AALREET?
ALRIGHT, SON...
...BUT ONE OF YOU STAYS 'ERE WITH ME. SECURITY, SEE.
URKAY.
NOW, DIWEN'T SHIT YER PANTS, SID. WE'LL BE REET BACK FOR YU, MAN...
...JUST GIVE US YER BANK ACCOONT NUMBER...
...AYE, AN' YER MUTHA'S MAIDEN NAME.
FOURTEEN HANDRED QUID. YOU'RE BACK WIV IT IN TEN MINUTES OR WE START DOIN' SAM FACKIN' DAMAGE TO SNOW WHITE 'ERE.
EXIT
NEXT EVENING...
FUCK! WELL, WUZ WAS AALL LUCKY IN LONDON...
AYE! I THOUGHT WE WAS GANNA GET W'HEEDS KICKED IN.
AYE!
PUBLIC BAR
AYE?...
...SOONDS LIKE SOME FUCKIN' ADVENCHA!...I WUNDA WHERE SID IS THE NEET. I'VE NOT SEEN 'IM SINCE YEEZ WENT T'LONDON.
ERM... AYE... I WUNDA.
AYE... ERM... ME AN'AALL.
WHY MAN, HE'LL BE...
COUGH! COUGH! ...A-HEM!
SKRIT! SKRIT!
REET. WHO'S ROOND IS IT?

M1 The North
Watford
1

THE END